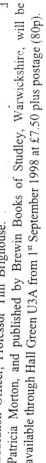

"THROUGH THE CLASS"

A book of schoolday memories from the 1920's, by members of the University of the Third . collection of old photographs, line drawings a Education Officer, Professor Tim Brighouse. Patricia Morton, and published by Brewin Books of Studley, Warwickshire, will be available through Hall Green U3A from 1st September 1998 at £7.50 plus postage (80p).

This book is a must for anyone who is interested in education, past or present, for anyone whose own childhood came within that period and a valuable resource for studying the sociology of wartime schooling. The writers come from a wide range of backgrounds, ranging from working class London to the peace and stability of the Earl of Bradford's estate in Weston-under-Lizard in Staffordshire. Many of the accounts do actually relate to Birmingham schooldays with a number of the writers going on to be Birmingham teachers and lecturers. The writer of "A Scientific Head Boy", for example, is a professor who held the chair of organic chemistry at the University of Birmingham for many years, having attended a city Primary School, a Birmingham Grammar School and the University of Birmingham. Many of these accounts are light hearted whilst others have a certain pathos. All are intriguing, arousing the reader's curiosity about the writer.

If you, or the group or organisation whom you represent, wish to order this book, please complete the form below and return it to:

Hall Green U3A TCW
21 Hollywood Lane
Hollywood
Wythall
Birmingham B47 5PT

All proceeds to U3A

Please send me .... copy/copies of "Through the Classroom Window"

Name ....

School, College or Organisation ....

Address ....

....

Tel No .... I enclose cheque/PO value £ .... inc p&p

THROUGH THE

CLASSROOM WINDOW

THROUGH THE CLASSROOM WINDOW

First published by
Brewin Books, Studley, Warwickshire, B80 7LG
in August 1998

ISBN 1 85858 123 0

British Library Cataloguing in Publication Data.
A Catalogue record for this book is available from the British Library

THROUGH THE CLASSROOM WINDOW

J. MORRIS and P. MORTON

Illustrations drawn by
John Farrell

ACKNOWLEDGEMENTS

The editorial committee of Hall Green U.3.A. offers special thanks to the twenty-three members who have created this collection of schoolday memories. These nine men and fourteen ladies have searched their minds and archives for material and photographs and we invite you to share in their recollections, both joyful and painful.

We also thank Professor Tim Brighouse for contributing his Foreword; John Farrell for his cover design and illustrations to the text; Ron Levy for providing the Index; Irene Mountford for hours of careful typing and Mr. K. A. F. Brewin for valuable support in the publication of this book.

CONTENTS

1. FOREWORD

Some people collect stamps, others antiques or old books. I confess I am a 'schoolaholic'. I always feel energised by visiting schools, especially when I am privileged to witness extraordinary and gifted teachers. Whenever that happens for me it is like listening to a superb piece of music, or witnessing a great innings at cricket.

So a book recalling school experiences is always going to appeal to me and this collection, some of which is written by distinguished Birmingham teachers, is no exception. Of course one of the appeals of such a book is to have reflections of one's own jostled into the forefront of the memory. For me it is the sharp contrast between attending a Midlands (not Birmingham) grammar school and hating every minute of it to such an extent that I was physically sick every morning before leaving home and then moving to a co-ed, sleepy grammar school after half a term when my father lost his job and we moved to Lowestoft on the east coast. The emblem on the cap was a rising sun and it reflected the warmth of the teachers and my fellow pupils. Immediately I was restored to normality. I saw what schools could be like and resolved to try to make all schools as welcoming and successful as that school was.

This book contains glimpses that will stir other people's memories, especially those of the Brummies who made the city what it is today. Teachers after all are the architects of our future.

Professor Tim Brighouse
Chief Education Officer
Birmingham LEA

William Cowper School
Newtown, Birmingham

2. INTRODUCTION

Schoolday Memories

Janet Morris

Our policy in Hall Green U.3.A. is to choose a broadly based theme in which to set our talks and visits over the year. Over a period of two years we focussed on the 19th and 20th centuries, which gave me an opportunity to research and talk about my own particular interest, the emergence and development of state education. As I prepared and delivered the talks I was well aware that in our diverse group there were people whose experience, knowledge and background in education went far deeper than mine. What I had not been prepared for was the wealth of personal anecdotes, considered opinion and strong memories that emerged from the group as a whole. As I listened and responded to people's questions and comments and talked to people afterwards, I felt certain that these rich memories should be written down, edited and collated in some form.

That we, as a group, would enjoy reading each other's contributions was a foregone conclusion. It seemed likely that other U.3.A. members from further afield would appreciate our efforts and identify with our experiences, but what we felt, above this, was the need to provide primary sources for the future; to record, whilst possible, experiences, attitudes, and emotions that are, in many respects, unique to our generation.

Those of us who have been, and still are, involved in education will appreciate the vast amount of change there has been, even in the last decade. Much of this will be officially recorded and documented, but the differences in emotional response and attitude can only be captured by the people themselves. We have something important to offer and the opportunity to do so gives us great pleasure.

In reading, editing and discussing the memories, certain themes seem to emerge. Firstly, there were the obvious difference between 'then' and 'now' – type of curriculum, school uniforms, style of buildings and modes of transport to and from school. Other things which emerged were more subtle and, in many ways, more interesting. One writer caught, simply and poignantly, the feelings of a small boy from a proud home as he experienced school on his first day. Would any child of today, we wonder, with the plethora of playgroups and nursery schools, be exposed to the rigours of all day school for the first time with such attention to smart new clothes and yet no attention to preparation for a new way of life?

Another writer pointed out the high intellectual quality of the teachers in his London Elementary school in the first part of this century, mainly because becoming a teacher, offered the only chance of higher education to bright children from poor homes – a fact we often forget.

Few of us will have appreciated, and hardly any of today's young adults will even know about, the life of a child in an orphanage boarding school. One contributor described her life as a boarder in the 1930s, allowing us to feel, just for a while, the austerity and rigid discipline governing the lives of quite young children.

A further thread that is woven through the accounts is the notion of the 11 plus or scholarship exam which children either passed or failed. Even those who went on to have successful careers retained that idea of failure if they went to Senior or Secondary Modern, as opposed to Grammar school. Wartime education clearly played an enormous part in the lives of our generation. To be uprooted from home and school with little or no warning and no idea of when (and if) they would return home must have been highly traumatic. No-one saw the need to counsel children or help them to come to terms with great change (no-one would have had time in such incredible conditions anyway) but most children appeared to survive admirably.

Finally, attitudes to teachers, adults and authority generally, were positive and largely unquestioning. A sense of shared values, a knowledge of right and wrong and views about religion, patriotism and Britain's place in the world were implicitly assumed to exist and were reflected in the teaching in schools. The lively, enquiring mind that must have questioned concepts such as 'authority' and 'patriotism' was still questioning quietly and privately as opposed to loudly and demandingly.

Hall Green U.3.A. members are delighted that Professor Tim Brighouse has agreed to write a foreword to this small collection of schoolday memories. His involvement is much appreciated and seems completely appropriate in view of the fact that many of our group are retired Birmingham teachers, lecturers or administrators and many more have had the privilege of a Birmingham education. As we look back to the past we also look forward to the future and congratulate Professor Brighouse on the tremendous improvements he has helped to bring about in the recent education of Birmingham children.

3. GETTING INTO THE SYSTEM

Wood Green, London in 1928

James Morton

There I stood, polished and shining, pressed and scrubbed from head to toe by the unrelenting hand of my diligent mother and enjoined firmly to stand still, while she put on her hat and made ready for the morning walk down the lane. Mother was rejoicing in our recent move to a new house, making it spick and span – immaculate – and her offspring must be likewise.

Not a time to float matchbox boats in the little stream. We were into serious business, my first day at school. There was no formal uniform required, only that enforced by practicality, strong footwear and sober hardwearing fabrics. But I was proud of the new outfit and admired my well shod feet occasionally on our way past gates and gardens.

Some mothers waited outside until the school bell should ring, trying to dislodge their limpet children and steer them through the great iron gates. This day my parent could escort me inside and I was glad of her nearness in the unfamiliar, nondescript gathering.

My domain, quickly allocated, proved to be one half of a dark oak table, scratched and grainy. Sliding into the seat, I turned to survey the other newcomers. Some still rueful and tearstained, refused to be comforted.

While looking for crayons and paper, I discovered a small pile of black slates, but the pencils squeaked so discordantly they were hastily discarded, and I moved on.

The slow minutes dragged till the bell rang sudden and sharp. Dinner! Time to go! Through the door and out. No mother waiting? I would go to meet her. Passing the park came temptation, there were fish in the round pond, should I turn in?

Triumphantly reaching home I marched up the garden path. The front door opened. All was not well. Consternation and a rapid turnabout into a speedy return and a quick trot through those heavy gates.

"We were looking for you" said a steely voice above my head.

4. CELANDINE DAYS

Our Village Life

Eleanor Hill

Looking back to my childhood days in a small village in the 1920's-1930's is like taking a journey back in time to a life so different from the present day that it seems like a distant dream.

Weston-under-Lizard straddles the A5, the old Roman Watling Street, and the village flanks the walls of the great manor house, Weston Hall, or Weston Park as it is now known to the thousands of visitors who go there each summer to enjoy the quiet beauty of the old estate and parklands.

It was very much more private in my childhood, in fact we thought it was the whole world for quite a long time, so complete was our life, without need or knowledge of wider fields.

A strange face gave cause for much comment and even concern, such as the arrival of a new policeman with his family, and it took a long time for such folk to be accepted as one of ourselves, although it usually happened eventually.

The village was self-supporting to a degree, as the estate employed the local people as tradesmen, gardeners, farm labourers and private servants.

Butchers and fishmongers sent their wares by van from nearby small towns and the baker's cart would make several journeys a week from Wheaton Aston, a village some four miles away, where the same family are still busily baking to this day.

Each month the tinker would arrive, with pots and pans hanging from his cart, a supply of paraffin for the oil lamps, and block salt which he cut into required lumps with a saw. I remember two pedlars; one wore plus-fours and rode a bicycle and sold liniment and white oils in small thin bottles, and we always bought one. The other pedlar walked, carrying his tray of wares around his neck. He was a huge man and wore a battered old trilby and a cloak. He sold laces, elastic, buttons, cottons, thread, needles, matches and sometimes Old Moore's Almanac. Heaven knows how many miles he walked each day.

Occasionally a barrel organ would pass through the village, it's owner like a Pied Piper of Hamelin, the children would long to follow him and sometimes did, only to be sent back in tears and tantrums.

The social life of the village centred mainly on the Church, and the School was used as a village hall for whist drives, dances, meetings, parties and concerts.

We had no public house in Weston and men who enjoyed a drink had to make a journey of several miles to The Bradford Arms or The Bell at Tong, both of which are still there today, looking much the same.

My Father was one of the village blacksmiths and had settled there after his return from Army service in France, and as a prisoner-of-war in Germany. He met Mother at a dance in Weston. She was a farmer's daughter from Herefordshire who worked at nearby Tong as a mother's help. Grandfather had come to Weston from Shrewsbury before the 1914-1918 war, and he and Father were stalwarts of the village choir, and both would sometimes sing at concerts. Father and his sister, my Aunt Mary, were members of the village choral society which was very successful in competitions around the Midlands, often winning banners.

This, then, is the backcloth for the days I would like to record as I remember them from my childhood, and as a tribute to the old friends who shared them with me so long ago.

School Days

My school days began in 1927, when I was 4½ years old. I remember clearly being taken along on the first day of the Summer term, feeling quite puffed up with pride and my own importance.

To break me in gently, I was allowed to sit with one of the senior girls whom I knew well as she lived in the village, and the day went very easily. Tuesday morning came and I was installed in my proper place in the infants' room with other little people, most of whom were strangers to me, as well over half of the pupils came in from areas around the village. Weston-under-Lizard school was typical of village schools of that time, under the wing of the Church, St. Andrews, but administered by Council authority. Our Headmistress, Mrs. Veasey and one assistant teacher, Mrs. Meek, looked after us all, and in my day the number of pupils on the roll was around 45.

The main part of the building took the senior and junior children and a curtain divided it from the infants' room. Infants sat at long desk benches and we had small slates with slate pencils to use for our early lessons. We vied with each other to learn to read quickly, and soon 'The cat sat on the mat' began to make sense and there was no holding us. Number work was not quite so popular but we had an early introduction to tables, which were learned by rote, and we gradually fell into the rhythmic reciting of them daily, with the result that we could call out the answers easily whenever we were tested.

Afternoons were for pleasant pursuits, i.e. drawing and modelling with clay using special tools, little bone-coloured knives and spatulas. We created African villages or Eskimo igloos, and modelled the animals we were familiar with at home. Our teachers seemed to be very fond of P.E., we had sessions of exercise frequently, and even on the coldest day had to gallop round the playground to 'improve our circulation'.

We became accomplished at country dancing and were sometimes invited to perform at other village halls. Infants also had to learn to stitch and I didn't really enjoy it. My coloured wool was often in a muddle and had to be sorted out, but my friend Kathleen was good at it and helped me a lot, as indeed she did all through school with knitting and sewing, in return for which I did all her drawing, it worked out very well for us both!

Lining the walls were bookcases, and the 'Blackie Readers' were our joy and didn't seem like hard work. We were often visited by a School Inspector and when I was about 6, he came one day, and as he sat down with us asked, "Who is the best reader here?" "I am", I replied, completely lacking in proper modesty. He always remembered and when he returned would ask, "Is the trumpeter still with us?" Each Tuesday the Rector came and we had extra religious lessons with him. He was an old bachelor gentleman with a beard, Mr. Rabone. He had a surprising way with children and we liked him, so Tuesdays were nice.

Music played a big part in our lives. Our Headmistress was a Graduate of Bangor University, steeped in music and the Arts, and it was our good fortune that she chose to spend three-quarters of her life in our village and share her fondness for music and literature with us. These were the days of the great British Empire, and each year we saluted the flag on Empire Day, May 24th, and sang patriotic songs in the playground:

"Pin your faith in the Motherland,"

"Land of Hope and Glory,"

"God bless the Prince of Wales."

We dressed up in various guises as Welsh, Scottish and Irish children, and gave readings on other lands that came under the Empire umbrella. Lord Bradford would join us with one or two of his daughters, and when all was finished he would invite us to spend the rest of the day in The Park, which we did with our usual gusto, climbing trees, chasing the deer, and paddling out to the moorhens' nests to see if they had any eggs or chicks, which they usually did.

Junior classes were a bit of a blow after the infant room, but we got down to it, mastered the art of pens and ink-wells, and with many blots, got going on the real nitty-gritty lessons. Essays were regular, we wrote them all the time, on many subjects and, if any of us went anywhere unusual, it was expected that we would write about it, and read it out to the other children.

Occasionally we all went somewhere unusual. One wonderful day we went to London with all the other children in Shropshire. We were taken by train, accompanied by the Member of Parliament for the Wrekin, who took us to the House of Commons, which was sitting at the time. We stood on the balcony beside the river Thames, little village children far from home, enjoying a whale of a day. We were taken sightseeing on London buses, and then to Regents Park Zoo. We had a lot to write about when we got back from that day out. Our M.P. later lost his life when he went down on the "City of Benares", evacuating children to Canada at the start of the war.

As a Church of England School, we had Ascension Day off after attending morning service, and sometimes had a picnic that day. One Ascension Day those of us who wished to, walked to Tong, a neighbouring village on the estate, some two miles away. We set off with our Headmistress and sang as we walked along Tong Lane, picking the odd dog-rose or honeysuckle here and there, and looking for birds' nests. When we reached the village, we paddled across a small stream, gasping as our toes sank into the wet, sandy bed, and looking out for sticklebacks. The picnic was a treat, as was being all together, and we sat under the oak trees with the sunshine dappling down on us. Afterwards we made our way to the village church. The old verger was expecting us, and showed us the grave of Little Nell, from Dickens' "Old Curiosity Shop". Next we saw the cannon-ball holes in the church wall from the days of the Civil War, and the other holes in the wall, where the lepers looked from their little room into the body of the Church.

At eleven we moved into the senior section of the schoolroom. Not much time now for fun and games, with only three years left to get prepared for life beyond the confines of our village cocoon. Several children were lucky enough to be able to go to Grammar School, but times were hard and it was not possible for many of us, even though we had passed the necessary examination. Two of my contemporaries, Maurice Dent and Charles Allman became Headmasters, Maurice from Grammar School and R.A.F. College, and Charles through the more difficult and long drawn out night school and Technical College route.

The last year at school brought for me a special task as the eldest girls prepared school dinners for the children who came in to the school from outside the village. It was always the same fare, thick bone and vegetable soup and a roly-poly or sponge pudding with custard. We cooked on an oil cooker, the only one I have ever seen, and it did valiant service over many years. We also prepared large jugs of cocoa and malted milk at break time in the winter which was very good. Children who were not very robust were given a spoonful of Virol each winter morning. I was always most careful never to need any! My friend Charles was not so lucky. After a bout of pneumonia he had to have a few doses. We even thought of breaking the jar of Virol so that he wouldn't have to take it, but didn't quite dare to.

I enjoyed the glory of being crowned May Queen by Lord Bradford in my final year and left school at the age of 14 with regret. I was grateful for the many good times, for the good basic grounding I had received there, and for the friendships, several of which were to be life-long, that had their roots there.

WESTON-UNDER-LIZARD SCHOOL in the early 1930s

Crowning the May Queen by the late Lord Bradford.

Electing a May Queen and dancing round the maypole are remnants of Sun worship, traceable to most ancient times.

Roman youths used to go into the fields dancing and singing in honour of Flora, Goddess of fruits and flowers. Later the English dedicated May Day to Robin Hood, because their favourite outlaw died on that day.

Juniors dancing in the schoolhouse garden.

Literally, "Through the Classroom Window". The Headmistress and friend in the early 1930's.

Senior Girls' Display – 1936

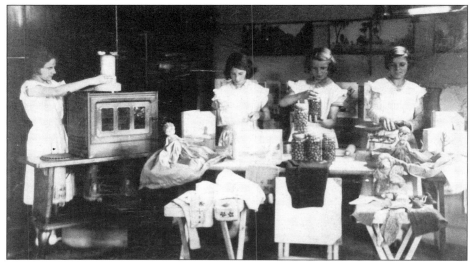

5. THE DANCING LESSONS

Janet Morris

'**N**o light between you and your partner, now, close together, moving as one!' Miss Gill's rich contralto rang out in the icy cold school hall. Twenty pairs of nervous sixteen year olds shuffled a little closer together, trying hard not to make eye contact with their partners. Miss Gill was five feet nothing in her tottery stilettoes. Her obviously dyed auburn hair formed a voluminous beehive on her head, her emerald green twinset, supporting a double row of artificial pearls, topped the tightly fitting maroon skirt and amazingly muscular, nylon clad legs.

She had a ferocious reputation for being able to teach anyone to ballroom dance but, more importantly in those days, she was also seen as the epitome of middle class gentility. The girls were 'gels' and the lads were 'young gentlemen', whether they liked it or not! Her eagle eyed chaperonage (hardly needed, I might add) was sufficient to comfort any parents who might have had misgivings about their daughters staying at school on winter evenings for 'mixed' activities.

By 1947 the war was well and truly over but the period of austerity was not. Fuel was in short supply, food was plain and not plentiful and clothing was still rationed, but gradually attitudes were changing. Our two grammar schools, Kings Norton Girls and Kings Norton Boys were just that; one foundation but, since 1927, two distinct buildings and two entirely separate communities. Hitherto the nearest we girls had got to the boys was on the 'bus, where a plethora of 'beret' flicking, satchel kicking and pigtail pulling broke out, unless a member of either staff was travelling. 'Berets' or caps were de rigueur and the 'no eating in public' rule was strictly enforced.

The most exciting thing that happened was the elimination of the 'bus stop at the end of Selly Oak Road, giving the girls the ideal excuse for walking along Northfield Road to catch the 'bus outside the Boy's School. Only the older girls wanted to do this since the younger ones preferred to live dangerously by walking to Cotteridge and trying to eat a surreptitious cream cake in the shadowy portals of The Watford Confectionery. For the fifteen year old upwards, the sight of the six foot prefects in ridiculous school caps controlling the 'bus queue at Northfield Road gave a particular kind of frisson. Berets were worn at a fashionable (and decidedly disapproved of) angle on the back of the head, the belts of navy 'gaberdines' were pulled dangerously tight and lisle stockings were worn inside out to give a prominent back seam. The occasional liaison was formed at the 'bus stop but, more often than not, it was a case of giggling, blushing and talking.

When it snowed, the windows of the Boys' lecture theatre were dragged open, snow scooped from the ledges and snowballs hurled down upon the hapless girls in the queue. Only the stern shouts of the duty prefects or the appearance (usually on a bike) of a tweedy, trilby hatted master, discouraged the onslaught. The two Heads, Miss Dynes and Mr. Reynolds had only the most formal contact but several girls in the school were daughters of masters in the Boys' School. Two such fathers, in particular, urged the Heads to allow greater co-operation between the two schools. Younger staff, both men and women, were returning from war service and the era of scholarly spinster school mistresses and the austere school master was soon to end.

Miss Dynes and Mr. Reynolds were approached by various staff groups and the question of ballroom dancing lessons was raised. Other joint activities were soon to follow for the fifth and sixth formers so that by the summer of 1948, we had an annual sixth form cricket match, a debating society and ultimately, a dance!! Nothing, however, made quite the impact of those dancing lessons. They were held on a Monday evening, starting immediately after school and ending at five o'clock. The Girls' School hall was large and airy and didn't have classrooms leading from it as did the Boys' hall so it was considered the best venue. The end of the school day heralded the end of the sparse heating so the hall was freezing. It was also dusty from several hundred feet during the day so the ambience was hardly glamorous, even without the drab, yellow lighting. The old gramophone provided the music since Miss Gill could hardly teach and play the Bechstein, even though, as she frequently assured us, she was more than capable of the latter.

We were not forced to attend 'BD' as we soon called it, but who could resist? There were rarely ever fewer than twenty girls and the same number of boys, many of whom turned up out of sheer curiosity. The thing to be dreaded most was an odd number of dancers because, horror of horrors, the odd girl or boy, was partnered by Miss Gill and became, excruciatingly, the exhibition dancer. The fifth formers only were invited to BD for reasons we never quite understood. Perhaps the small exclusive coterie of sixth formers claimed pressure of work, and I know that when I attained the dizzy heights of Lower Sixth, I never enquired why we weren't invited to BD.

The first lesson was scheduled for the week before half term. The mirrors in the toilet block attracted a long queue of would be dancers with combs, hair grips and slides and the urgent need to coax hair into 'bangs', 'page boys' and the odd 'slinky wave'. Blow drying was unheard of and hairstyles were fixed and formal, needing a fair amount of 'underpinning'. The odd bottle of cheap perfume was passed around, sensible lace-ups were 'polished' with form room dusters, stocking seams were viciously straightened and finger nails were frantically filed. At last we shuffled, coyly, through the double doors into the hall. At the other end were a group of embarrassed looking boys, well combed and with brushed blazers and straightened ties.

Our first emotion was disappointment because these were, of course, only the fifth formers and they seemed young and small. The prefect heroes of seventeen were sadly absent and we really had no choice but to 'put up' with the 'children'. Miss Gill swept through the main door like a stately galleon, bosom heaving and beehive balancing aloft. Of the nervous huddles she would have none and immediately ordered us to surround her, whereupon, in the blink of an eye, she had girl matched to boy in no uncertain manner. Not a soul giggled or even smiled. We were to learn the waltz, but to commence, each 'young gentleman' must say to his 'gel' "May I have the pleasure of this dance?" The 'gel' should then say, "Thank you, I would love to" (Young of the millennium eat your hearts out!) The fact that we were already standing ready paired and with no option mattered not one jot.

There followed an hour of solemn 'one-two-three-ing' which, later, was accompanied by "I'll be with you in apple blossom time" on the gramophone. In later weeks we quick-stepped, slow fox-trotted and tangoed to something approaching an acceptable standard. To this day I can't go to a dance (or disco as it usually is) without remembering Miss Gill and the lad with acne who usually headed my way. We all became fond of the medley we called "Annie get your Oklahoma", not really knowing which bit came from what musical. All we knew was that Elizabeth and Philip danced to "People will think we're in love" and that gave the whole thing an aura of pure romance.

In fact very few teenage romances did emerge from the BD group, as our elders may naturally have feared, but a few treasured friendships did. Walking to the 'bus stops or wheeling bikes up Selly Oak Road in the dark enabled girls and boys to chatter freely, now released from the painful formality of the dancing. Most of the chatter was jokes about Miss Gill and bizarre fantasies about liaisons between members of the teaching staffs.

A few years ago I was invited to meet the father of my successor as Head of an Infant School. As we approached each other to shake hands our howls of mutual recognition were followed by "Can you still tango?" – We were both, indeed, protégés of Miss Gill's ballroom dancing lessons!

6. SCHOOLDAYS – A QUAINT WORLD

Eileen Miller

My school career started soon after the outbreak of war although we lived sufficiently far from any action which might have disrupted my progress. One of the earliest memories I retain is linked to the unpleasant smell associated with the inside of a gas mask which had to be worn on the odd occasions we were involved in practice trips to the air-raid shelters. I attended three different primary schools and sat the new 11 plus examination in the third establishment, having arrived in a new town just in time to start the final year.

The change of circumstances did not prevent me from gaining a place at one of the girls' grammar schools which I entered full of enthusiasm and expectation. There were exciting new subjects called French, Latin and German, and opportunities to take part in music and drama festivals both locally and regionally. There were also organised visits to professional theatre productions and foreign films. My horizons were broadened considerably and we were also encouraged to develop our levels of self-confidence by being chosen to speak or recite at public occasions such as speech days.

The school was set in its own extensive grounds and our physical, as well as our intellectual development was well catered for. As I enjoy my swimming today, I am eternally grateful for the tuition I was forced to undergo all those years ago under the steely eye of a former Olympic competitor. Standards of conduct were also emphasised and it goes without saying that we were all fully uniformed. A hat was worn on the journey to and from school and, on arrival, the first duty was to change from outdoor to indoor shoes. We were discouraged from associating with the opposite sex to the extent that the annual Christmas party was an all-female affair including printed dance programme which had to be filled in with the required number of names.

The teaching staff were a well-qualified and largely committed group of mainly single women with the exception of one poor male who struggled manfully to keep control. With the odd exception, discipline presented few problems and the majority of girls left at the age of 16, with a small élite staying on in the 6th form and destined for higher education. It was a period during which firm friendships were forged, some of which endure to the present day, whilst, at the same time, petty jealousies surfaced from time to time to create ripples on the calm surface.

One particularly vivid memory is linked to the long and severe winter of 1947. We were allowed to walk to the nearby park where the lake had been transformed into a block of solid ice. The majority of us stood at the edge and watched enviously as those of our classmates who had learned to skate gave an enchanting exhibition of grace and artistry and the picture remains with me to this day.

Looking back through contemporary eyes, I see a somewhat quaint world of school set in the aftermath of war and still untroubled by major educational upheaval. With hindsight, I reckon I was fortunate to be in the right place at the right time.

7. WHEN THE MAY IS IN BLOSSOM

Andrea Applebe

Hartfield Crescent – 1935-37

'Next year when the May is in blossom, you'll be going to school', was mother's reply to my constant question as we walked along Fox Hollies Road to the shops on the boulevard. I was eager and enthusiastic to join my brother Tony who had started the previous autumn. He had been my constant companion for as long as I could remember and I missed him. He would come home with what he had done at school and I wanted to join in.

The long awaited day arrived in the summer term of 1935. I was just five years old. My mother took me along to meet the other children, all standing around the small playground of Hartfield Crescent School. She gave me a brief kiss, patted me on the head, told me to be a good girl and do as I was told and was gone. I stood there wondering what was going to happen, a bit miserable and feeling let down. Soon, Miss Uzzal, the reception teacher gathered us all up and took us into the classroom. Miss Uzzal was tall, slim with dark hair and wasn't very old. She was very pleasant and told us all to sit down. The classroom seemed huge and was furnished with small tables and chairs. She took my hand and putting it into the hand of another child said, "Will you do something for me? Will you look after this little girl who is very upset?" With that, she sat me down beside the little girl who was sobbing her heart out. So began my career of 'taking-care' of people which has lasted all my life one way or another. The little girl's name was Kathleen and she lived in the same road as I. We became constant companions and our friendship lasted until the war and evacuation separated us.

I don't remember much of the routine in those early days, except that we were taught some of the social graces, to say 'please' and 'thank you' and also to sit down when asked. Morning milk time was a rather serious affair. We all had to sit very quietly whilst it was handed out and drunk. Those children who had brought something to eat during break had to have a paper plate so as not to make a mess spilling the crumbs. Afternoons were spent in recreation or play, drawing, crayoning, stencilling, large jig-saws etc. I seemed to have spent most of my time threading glass beads on a

rather hairy string. The beads were blue, green and amber and came in a small thick heavy cardboard box which tipped over very easily much to my consternation. I spent most of my time scrabbling on my hands and knees picking them up.

The school day was from 9.00 a.m to 12 noon in the morning, and from 2.00 p.m. to 4.00 p.m. in the afternoon. Very few children were taken to or collected from school. Most of us had to make our own way there and back and we were seen across Fox Hollies Road by our policeman. He appeared very big, particularly with his helmet on, but he was very friendly and took great interest in all the children. He knew our names, shared our sweets, wished us 'Happy Birthday' and of course listened to all our trials and tribulations at school. He was our friend and protector!

In the autumn term of 1935 I moved up to Miss Dodsworth's class. She too, was dark haired, but a bit plumper and older. Here I learned to read. My first book was the proverbial 'The Cat Sat on the mat', in black and white. It cost one penny (old pence). The front was covered with pictures of black and white cats and the print was big and bold.

I read quickly and easily, moving through the readers quite quickly with very few problems, except with one book which caused me some difficulty in distinguishing 'farmhouse' and 'famous'. These two words confused me but not half as much as when I first encountered silent letters! I must have been introduced to phonics and one of my books was entitled 'Tommy's Island'. I can remember having a terrible argument with my mother over the pronunciation of island. 'How can it be i-land when there in an 's' in it?' I argued. My poor mother gave up in the end. 'Oh, have it your way', she said in sheer desperation. Even in those early days I took a lot of convincing and evidently had a mind of my own!

It was in Miss Dodsworth's class that I received my first smack. We had desks with tip up seats and we were all standing on them reciting a poem. I had a gob-stopper in my pocket and I took it out, I suppose to have a quick suck. Unfortunately I dropped it and of course I got down to retrieve it. For this disobedience I had my legs smacked and what was worse, the gob-stopper was confiscated!

My first Christmas at school has stayed with me all my life. We were ushered into the dimly lit hall, where standing floor to ceiling was the largest and most wonderful Christmas tree I had ever seen. It shimmered and shone and danced with light. I had never seen anything like it. The children began to sing 'Away in a Manger'. I was overwhelmed with emotion and to this day whenever I hear 'Away in a Manger' my eyes fill and I remember that first Christmas at school.

I made good progress and was soon moved up again even though I was still only six years of age. this time into Miss Read's class. She was fair haired, older than Miss Dodsworth and I didn't like her. She was a strict, severe teacher with a sharp angry voice and very little patience. In her class I learned to write using pen and ink and literally blotted my copy book. We had ruled our margins in our brand new exercise books and were told to copy the date from the blackboard. No one had forewarned me about the properties of pen and ink, either that or I had not been listening! I, enthusiastically dipped the pen into the inkwell and in transferring pen to paper, – splat, a large ink blot appeared in the middle of my page! I was horrified. Miss Read was extremely angry, smacked my legs for making a mess, and what was worse, tore the page out of my book in front of the whole class. I was hot with shame and embarrassment. I never forgave her and it was during my stay in her class that I began to have a fear and dislike of school. I used to feel sick and have bilious attacks, but there was no escape, I was still sent to school.

My last teacher at Hartfield was Miss Whittingham. She was much older than most of the other teachers. She wore her hair in a bun and used to come to school on a bicycle. She was much kinder and had a greater understanding of children than Miss Read. She restored my faith and confidence in school which had been so badly shaken by Miss Read. The coronation of George VI took place whilst I was in her class and we had a wonderful time stringing up the red, white and blue buntings, painting and drawing in honour of the occasion, and of course, receiving our Coronation Mugs. July 1937 saw the end of my schooldays at Hartfield. A new era began in September of that year.

York Road (now York Mead) – 1937-41

A brand new school! – No child had ever used any of the equipment, nor sat in any of the desks – everything brand new – nothing had been used – a unique experience. The school had been built on an allotment site in York Road and was finished ready for the first intake in September 1937. It had eight classrooms – four for infants (including the reception class) and four for the juniors. It was an entirely new concept in design with lots of glass and doors running full length of the classroom which opened out on to lawns and flower beds. It was light and airy – a far cry from the 1920's building of Hartfield Crescent.

Miss Condrey was the Headmistress. I suppose she must have been in her late fifties. She was short and stocky with pepper and salt hair and a peppery temperament to match. You either liked or loathed her. From the start she was determined that her school – her brand new school would be the best and strove hard to achieve it. She had a rather Churchillian stance but she resembled her terrier (Billy) more than a bulldog!

There were tables and chairs instead of desks in the juniors. Each pupil had a large box which fitted under the table and which contained wooden numbers, single and stacks of ten counters glued together as aids to understanding maths. Also included was a box of 144 square inches for area. We were taught maths in 'concrete terms', i.e. for each operation we had to put the numerals out on the table and alongside the appropriate number of counters. These were then added, subtracted, multiplied or divided using both single counters and multiples of ten, so that you knew exactly what you were doing and what had taken place. In the same way, area was demonstrated, first covering the space with square inches, and then, by counting and then multiplying, developed the concept of area. I learned to do $Pi(\frac{22}{7})$ in exactly the same way. There was a large circle painted in the middle of the playground and by using a large piece of rope we measured the diameter in relation to the circumference and hence established the ratio between the two measurements. She established a very mathematical knowledge and once learned, these concepts were never forgotten. We learned our tables by rote and had daily mental and spelling tests to keep us on our toes as well as a lot of problem solving. Great emphasis was also put on reading and writing. Most days we had a silent reading period and we were encouraged to borrow books from the extensive class library. We learned about the production of every day commodities, paper, cloth, tea, coffee, cocoa etc, with the aid of a flickery black and white cine projector. Our interests in nature were stimulated by growing peas and beans, mustard and cress under controlled conditions. We also listened to a B.B.C. broadcast called, if I remember correctly, 'Out with Romany'. The arts were not forgotten – as well as painting and drawing (using board and easel) we experienced the use of drawing with charcoal (messy) and also calligraphy.

Each Friday afternoon we assembled in the hall for singing practice. Usually it included all the folk songs, 'Caller Herring', 'Annie Laurie', 'Ha Weel May the Keelrow'. I never understood many of the words for as you can gather, a lot were in a broad Scot's dialect. Country dancing was also on the curriculum, and many an hour was spent puffing our way through 'Sir Roger de Coverley' and 'The Virginian Reel'. – All this sounds wonderful, but there was a snag – you had to be bright and eager to learn, if not, Miss Condrey was not interested.

I began in September 1937 in class five. Miss McDougall, a plump motherly teacher came from Australia. She kept us entertained for hours by recalling her memories of her homeland and by her vivid and graphic readings of 'Rikki Tikki Tavi'. We were enthralled by her performance. Unfortunately she didn't stay long – I expect she was shipped back to Australia as somehow or other I felt she didn't fit in with Miss Condrey's ideas.

In 1938 I moved up into class seven – skipping class six – I don't know why – perhaps I had potential. Miss Trenouth was in charge and she was different as chalk and cheese both in manner and appearance from what I had experienced with any previous teachers. She was dark haired with a cottage loaf figure. She wore very colourful clothes, particularly in the summer, her dresses had large bright patterns and she wore high-heeled shoes, sometimes slingbacks! What was even more startling, she wore make-up AND nail polish!!! We children thought we had a movie star in the school. She was pleasant and seldom shouted, but nevertheless, she was a firm disciplinarian. Later, during the war, she married – a rather handsome naval lieutenant – whom all the girls thought very dashing – and still retained her job. She taught me to knit and I was extremely proud of my first Pixie Hood knitted entirely in garter stitch. Her favourite project was the embroidery of a set of curtains for the staff room. These consisted of appliquéd daffodils on to a dark brown background. We spent hours pinning, tacking and buttonholing these fiddly bits of daffodils on to the cloth. You can be sure that we always remembered our knitting or sewing for needlework classes!

A school trip was organised together with Smith's Coaches to take a party to the Cheddar Gorge and Weston-super-Mare during the summer term of 1938. The cost was seven shillings and sixpence – payable at a rate of sixpence a week. Most of the parents were not well off and it was quite an item to afford. However, I was lucky enough to go. It was my first trip on a coach and my first experience of the sea. (I had never had a holiday). As usual, the tide was out and the muddy flats were somewhat of a let down, but I shall always remember the smell of the sea. The cost of the trip included lunch and tea at Fortes – called, if I remember correctly, Fortes Tea Rooms – the forerunner of the now nationwide Fortes Restaurants. We were all suitably impressed by its decor and the fountain in the forecourt. A second trip to Rhyl was organised for 1939 which I also enjoyed, but this was the last as war loomed on the horizon and put an end to many of the school activities.

By the end of 1939 I had moved into the top class. I was one of the youngest in the class – most of the children were two years my senior. I came third from the bottom in the end of the year exams, but by the next year, I was in the top three. We were all being coached for what came to be known as the eleven-plus exam. Miss Condrey's aim was to get as many children into grammar school education as possible. During the time she was headmistress, she had a hundred per cent success rate with two or three achieving scholarships for King Edwards. We had to gain a scholarship because our parents in the main could not afford the fees for grammar school education. She was very successful, but of course, she handpicked the children who were going to sit the exam.

In October 1940, I took my exam at College Road (now Springfield Road) school, after spending all night in the air-raid shelter, for by now it was the height of the blitz and most nights we endured the attentions of the Luftwaffe.

At one time, there was no water, gas or electricity. My brother and I fetched water from the artesian well at Joseph Lucas. (Ever tried pushing a dolly tub of water in a pram up hill and then hanging on to it going down another?) It was not unusual, when on our way to school, to be confronted with a barrier and a sign 'Danger – unexploded bomb – detour', we didn't seem to worry – took it in our stride and followed the detour signs.

It was decided because of the continuing raids and difficult conditions that the school should be evacuated. So, early one cold November morning, we all set off, tagged, complete with gas masks, a few possessions and a rolled up blanket on our train journey to Wales. We arrived in Ogmore Vale (not far from Bridgend) a typical grey coal mining village in the late afternoon. My two sisters, Ann (aged eight) and Roslyn (just over five years old) were left standing on the station as it was difficult to place three children in one family. It was decided that Roslyn and I should stay together, for obvious reasons – I could take care of my younger sister, and Ann was to be billeted separately. It turned out that we were in the same street, only a few doors away from each other.

It was an unhappy and difficult experience for me. I didn't get on with my foster mother. She was sharp tongued and waspish (echoes of Miss Read?)

and her two daughters made my life unbearable with their catty remarks and spiteful behaviour. I also had the responsibility of Roslyn, who really was very young to be away from home. All in all, life was very difficult.

We were sent to the local school. Again an experience we could have all done without. It was ruled, and I mean ruled, by Miss Wheeler, a forbidding, stern figure, whom we had to call 'Governess'. Silence and obedience were the rules that governed the school. We stood in silence whilst waiting to go into the classroom and stood whenever a teacher entered. Although discipline was very harsh, the standard of education was excellent. I learned the metric system which has stood me in good stead and quite a bit of Welsh. I said that Miss Wheeler frightened the life out of us – that was in school. Roslyn and I had a long walk to school in all winds and weathers and most mornings we met Miss Wheeler. Out of school she was a different person entirely. She was very friendly, talked and chatted, and even made jokes, but as soon as she entered the school gate a different persona emerged.

I endured my stay in Ogmore for a long five months – release came in March when my mother and father visited us and I begged them to take us home. Ann was much happier with her foster parents. She was the only girl in a houseful of boys and had a lot of attention. She decided to stay behind and didn't return home until July.

Mr. Carter, one of our teachers, had also been evacuated but had returned to Birmingham a couple of months previously. I ended my last year in his class. He was of medium height, fair, with a good sense of humour. He was married with a little girl called Marion, whom we knew, and this made him more understanding. He was the first male teacher I had had. I was not intimidated by him being a man and on the whole enjoyed my stay in his class. I learned that I had won a scholarship to Yardley Grammar School. This meant that my books and fees were paid for a year – just as well as my parents were at that time not in a position to pay for my education. My future for the time being seemed secure. My days at York Road quickly drew to a close. On the last day I went up on the platform to receive a prize and congratulations for my hard work and achievements – such as they were (I didn't think I had done a lot). I had enjoyed my life at York Road and look back on it as one of the happier times of school life.

8. THE BOOK COVERER PAR EXCELLENCE

Ann Marsh

In 1938 I started at the local State School in York Road, Hall Green, which was built in 1937. The reception class had a huge walk-in dolls' house, complete with furniture, cups and saucers and a teapot. I arrived home one day with two head lice walking down the parting in my hair! The school hours were 9-12 and 2-4 p.m.

When I was eight, our school was evacuated to Ogmore Vale in Wales, as we had suffered some heavy bombing and were without water, gas or electricity, and had several broken windows. The journey seemed to take all day as we were shunted onto other tracks due to bomb damage. We arrived late at night, complete with name tabs, and carrying a blanket and a small bag of clothing. I was billeted with a family who were kind to me and I attended the local school on the other side of the valley. They taught us songs in the Welsh language, which I have since forgotten. On occasions I was late for school and would creep in to the cloakroom during assembly and join the others on their way to class. My lateness was due to poor supervision. Mrs. Davies, my foster mother, would remain in bed long after I went to school so I had to get my own breakfast. Emlyn, the youngest of the family, would play cards with me (Snap!) which made me late for school.

The house was on a steep hill, one of the many in a ribbon type arrangement. There was no bathroom, just a tin bath in the parlour. There was just one cold water tap without a sink, just a bucket underneath. The toilet at the end of the garden was just a dry privy, no light, and sheets of newspaper on a string for use! Sheep would get in to the garden and eat the vegetables should anyone fail to lock the gate which they often did. I was always blamed for this!

My education really came to a full stop for almost a year. On my return, a nervous, anxious child, I failed to catch up, living in fear and dread of one teacher who was very moody. I soon learned to recognise her bad days because then she wore red!

The only activities I was good at were dancing, gym and covering books. My own text books were covered with samples from a wallpaper book. We all had a text book each to cover the various subjects. The headmistress raised money to help buy them by holding Bridge evenings. I was very good at book covering, being neat and quick, and I would help out those less adept – this made me popular.

My position in class was towards the bottom, which I shared with a boy I sat with on the back row. He had troublesome dandruff and would rub his head, scattering the dry skin on to the desk. We would collect this in little piles and compare our harvest with previous weeks! One girl who sat in front of us had long black plaits, which we poked into the ink well – she didn't seem to mind! All the inkwells had to be washed every Friday afternoon and our desks inspected.

I failed my 11+ – I wasn't worried – and went to the local Secondary Modern School, Harrison Barrow in Hartfield Crescent. I enjoyed this school and caught up and found myself always in the first three in the class. I was introduced to classical music by the Headteacher. Each morning she would play a record after Assembly and would tell us something about it every day. Each week we would have a different record and at the end of the month a test. I always got 100%. My other interests were P.T., hockey, netball, dancing, cookery and art. The latter I excelled in. I became School Captain in my final year and left at the age of 15 to study at Evening Classes (called Night School) where I learned short-hand and typing and other valuable subjects during the next three years.

9. ONE OF THE COPPER BAND

Margaret Grubb

Since volunteering to write this account I have been dismayed to learn that because I failed the grammar school entrance examination, I was considered to be in the copper band of educational ability. However, life is a learning process, so here goes!

I was born in 1935 and my parents and I moved to my present address when I was six months old. I only attended local schools so did not travel great distances for tuition.

I went to Chapel Fields Infant and Junior School (which, incidentally, celebrated its 60th birthday this year (1998) and is less than a mile from my home). I have few memories of my schooling there, particularly the infant years as I had quite a few childhood illnesses. During the years I was at the Junior School the Headteacher was a Mr. W. K. Neville. I think he stayed there until he reached retirement age.

I can remember three teachers, namely Mrs. Smith, Mrs. England and Miss Glover, the latter two were my third and fourth year form teachers. I think Miss Glover was also Deputy Headteacher and that she, too, remained at the school until she attained retirement age.

I do not remember the school celebrating the end of the Second World War, although street parties were held in the road I live in for both VE Day and VJ Day.

Three memories of that time that come to mind are: – Playing truant for part of an afternoon with a girl named Jean Jordan to go blackberrying, and having to explain myself to the teacher afterwards! – When I was in the fourth year and in charge of a dinner table for eight children, sending one or other of them to collect the meals but having the choice of second helpings first. I was not alone in this practice and am sure I took the lead from someone else! – Going down into an air raid shelter sited at the edge of the playground; sitting on a bench and singing 'Ten Green Bottles'. I think this must have been a practice drill rather than an actual air raid.

I remember my mother making me a green and white checked dress but am unsure whether this formed part of a school uniform.

I commenced my secondary education at Lode Heath County Modern School, Lode Lane, Solihull (as it was then known) in September 1946 and I left in July 1950.

If a girl passed the 11+ examination she went to Malvern Hall High School for Girls, Brueton Avenue, Solihull (now St. Martin's School). My friend from schooldays tells me one girl in our class sat the 12+ examination and transferred to the grammar school. I wonder how she managed it as to me she was too slow to catch a cold.

At the time, Lode Heath was under the jurisdiction of Warwickshire County Council at Warwick: Solihull Metropolitan Borough Council being formed in 1964. I think there was only one other county modern school in the Solihull area then, namely Sharmans Cross at Shirley. I know that in one direction the catchment area for Lode Heath school extended as far as Hampton-in-Arden and in another to Sheldon.

It was (and still is) a mixed school and classes stayed together for most subjects. There were four School Houses, namely Kingsbury (Blue), Avon (Red), Arden (Green) and Dunsmore (Yellow) to which I belonged. Naturally, we had pride in them and there was fierce rivalry in competitions and pleasure when house points were earned.

We had a school uniform which we were expected to adhere to as far as possible. You had to have a good reason for not wearing it. As clothing coupons were still in force most of us had only one set of clothing so some pupils smelt a little by Friday afternoon! When a girl's hair was a certain length it had to be tied back. You were not allowed to wear jewellery.

We had school prefects and I was for the latter part of my school life Vice-Captain of the girl prefects. I didn't get to be Head Girl because the Captain at that time left after me! I believe in those days pupils left at the end of the summer, autumn and easter terms depending on when you reached the age of 15 years.

If you lived three miles or more from the school and did not have a bicycle of your own, you could have one on loan from the school. Mine was a black sit-up and beg affair with L155 stamped on the handlebar. It was returned when I left school. The Midland Red bus company ran a school bus service specially for the school. I think there were two buses run in the morning and the same number in the afternoon. When we had had a cookery lesson, I did not enjoy going home after school with a Lancashire Hot Pot in a lidless pyrex dish!

We had a gymnasium and I hated using the wall-bars and climbing ropes. I didn't mind trying to go over the horse or running along the low benches. Boys and girls were separated for sports. We played netball and rounders but were not taught how to swim or play tennis. We were taught some country dances.

To play rounders or do field events we had to walk a little way down Lode

Lane, say 300-400 yards, in our navy blue knickers, white blouses and plimsolls! There were separate changing rooms adjoining the gym and two people had to hold a black curtain so the boys would not see us running through the showers. You had to have a good reason for not taking a shower. There was a school football team and a girls' rounders team and once a year there was a match between them and the teachers.

I thought most of our teachers were quite old. This was probably due to the war. However, my friend's sister (who went to a grammar school) said the teaching given to us was in line with a grammar school. Some younger teachers joined the staff in the last two years of my schooling. I believe they had done the two-year crash course.

In the Autumn of the years 1948-49 we went potato picking for which we were paid something like £1.0s.0d each time. The first year we went to a farm at Bacons End and the second year to one at Hockley Heath.

There was a Chess/Draughts Club, a Poetry Group, neither of which I joined, and a school choir which I was asked to leave!!!

We had two school outings, one to London (for which I think I saved 30/- at the rate of 1/- per week) and one to New Brighton. During my final year a party did go to Paris for a week but I did not join them.

There was a library but I do not remember using it. We were not taught any languages or to read any of Shakespeare's plays. I remember plodding through poems/epics such as The Charge of the Light Brigade, The Lady of Shalott, Morte d'Arthur and the Rhyme of the Ancient Mariner. I had trouble with the pronunciation of 'Abu' when reciting the poem 'Abu Ben Adhem' and was sent out of the classroom. We had musical appreciation once a week but I never attended a concert outside school. My friend Marina remembers going to a concert at Birmingham Town Hall and hearing Isobel Baillie sing.

When I was in my third year the girls were sent to learn woodwork and the boys cookery. I cut my left thumb with a chisel whilst making a table mat. I still remember the smell of a simmering pot of fish glue.

Although we were taught needlework I never completed anything!

Half a day was spent on careers' advice (at the time I expressed a wish to work for the Britannic Assurance Company but I never worked for them). As commercial subjects were not taught, along with several other girls I went privately for shorthand and typing lessons.

We did not have a tuck shop but in a latter part of my time at Lode Heath we could sometimes buy small packets of biscuits for 2d. I believe we were also given one or two tins of cocoa powder. At one time we had free school milk in ½ pint bottles. Some mornings during the winter (maybe 1947) it was frozen.

There was a period during the winter of 1947 when we were unable to go to school because of the heavy falls of snow.

I cannot recall any school group photographs being taken but I have one or two solo pictures of me. A photographer came to the school and one sat on a school bench with a brick wall as a backdrop.

I recently looked through a school magazine produced in 1951. I am sure one was not published whilst I was there.

The school celebrated its 50th birthday in 1989 but I did not go to the celebrations held at the George Hotel, Solihull. Over the years there have been a few reunions of the girls in my form. The last one held was in April 1995 when we all attained our 60th year. Eighteen of us met and we had a meal, with a celebratory cake, at the Regency Hotel, Solihull.

I left school at the age of 15 years with only the standard end of year report.

10. SCHOOLDAYS IN WEMBLEY

Stan Miller

It was my wife's eagle eye that spotted the advertisement in the copy of the Saga magazine that we had received, unsolicited, while I was away on business last year (1997). My former secondary school, a mixed grammar school in the northwest suburbs of London and now amalgamated with two other schools to form Alperton Community School, was to celebrate the 75th anniversary of its foundation. The invitation to all former pupils to attend the gathering was intriguing; I had set foot in that seat of learning only once in the 46 years since I completed my seven years of …? well, let's say seven years of attendance, that's neutral enough!

Whatever else may be said about the former Wembley County School, the organisation of this re-union was impressive. Some 900 people attended, I was told, and classrooms were allocated to decades (e.g. 1940-49 entry) where photos, past and present, plus name labels, facilitated the recognition of otherwise total strangers as long-lost companions of the journey towards truth and enlightenment! It was a strange business picking up the threads with people you had last seen nearly 50 years ago and whose very existence had escaped your attention since then!

I was really quite gratified to be recognised by more than one former school-mate but, alas, not for my erudition nor for my immense contribution to the life of the school but for ice-hockey, my consuming passion in those days, the practice of which, during out of school hours, was certainly a major contributor to my embarrassing failure at A level in my two main subjects!

Schooldays, therefore, have been brought to mind this year. Conversations on that day in May and in subsequent communication with former school friends now resident in the USA, whose whereabouts were brought to light on that occasion, have prompted a search for old photos and a re-awakening of memories.

What I remember most clearly about my Primary schooldays was the fact that the two storey building, with Infants on the ground-floor and Juniors upstairs, was set on a hillside adjacent to a park. Beneath the building, to the rear, were the rain-shelters with wooden benches round the walls, where you could take refuge either from the rain or from that tall well-built Bernard Br......, the school bully, during playtimes. Not for long, however, because, with the onset of war, the rain-shelters became the air-raid shelters by the simple expedient of erecting a brick wall to enclose them. It was here that I spent many, many hours of my early education, safe in the knowledge that I was protected from bombs falling in the locality but oblivious to the fact that a direct hit on the school would have caused it to engulf all of us seated "safely" below!

We stayed in our London suburb throughout the blitz and the arrival of the V1 doodle bugs but when a V2 rocket landed a $1/4$ of a mile from home, the Miller family decamped to the relative safety of the temporary home of an aunt in Northampton. So it was that I began my secondary education as a member of the ad hoc Middlesex Evacuated Grammar School which operated in the dilapidated premises of a former Elementary school at the backend of town. A severe drought, with water fetched in buckets from mobile tankers; sharing a room with my brother and two cousins for whom our dislike was only matched by theirs of us; my early lessons in French using a text-book which was modern and enlightened 100 years previously, constitute my principal recollection of these mercifully brief few months.

The highlights of my almost seven years at Wembley County are few – although allocated to the A stream (largely, I think, based on an expectation performance in line with my older brother) I achieved little academic distinction, even before joining the Wembley Junior ice-hockey team, and came to teachers' notice as much because of stupid behaviour in Science lessons as for any kind of solid achievement. (Rather a good preparation, I think, for a future teacher and school inspector).

The silliness in Science lessons came home to roost, however, when, many years later, having succeeded in getting a couple of school text-books published, I sat in a sparsely attended meeting of the Educational Writers Group of the Society of Authors opposite a lady whom, I realised, was the same person who had attempted to teach me Science and who, years later, at the age of 89, was the driving force in the organisation of the May 1997 re-union.

Our Headmaster, who had "opened" the school in 1922, had a well-established reputation in the locality: aloof, begowned and adept in the use of the cane, he was, thankfully, a remote distant figure who retired early in my time at the school. He was replaced by a younger but not much more engaging person in the eyes of his pupils. An accomplished Morris dancer, he would demonstrate his prowess in this field, suitably attired in bells and hat, to the "delight" of all his pupils and, I guess, his staff! Ever mindful of the importance of cultural development, he introduced a number of special events at which the whole school was assembled to witness a performance by an eminent musician; the bassoonist Archie Camden was one such artist but the performance which none of us will forget (and, clearly, those at the re-union still had fresh in their minds) was that given by the Dolmetsch ensemble, specialists in early music using authentic instruments. For youngsters in the mid 1940s, the majority from fairly "ordinary" suburban homes, attentive listening to that kind of music for more than a few minutes was too great a challenge to conformity and, sure enough, our normal discipline broke down and the performance had to be brought to a premature and less than dignified end. What followed was a three year reign of terror during which we were marshalled round the school in complete silence at all times with no relaxation of what seemed to us to be a prison regime. I don't think that did much to further my musical education but it did point to the importance of the principle of "fitness for purpose".

Although I usually enjoyed learning French and German, I was quite happy to join with my classmates in my Fourth year in persuading our new young Languages teacher to depart from the splendours of the French Subjunctive Mood to tell us about his recent adventures as an interpreter to Field-Marshal Montgomery at the German surrender on Luneburg Heath. I eventually mastered the Subjunctive at University but still remember those fascinating insights, recalled when, last May in that crowded W.C.S. classroom, I met that same "young" teacher, now in his 80s, who suggested that he hadn't really succeeded with us but did rather better later in his career … I wonder!?

Swimming lessons, early morning single periods spent largely in the 10 minute coach ride each way to the open-air pool, in which I never did overcome my fear of the water; Wednesday lunch-hours in the Upper school when we learnt ball-room dancing, including the formalities of "May I have the pleasure …" in the context of full school uniform and, finally, my abrupt departure at the end of the week I completed my A levels in order to start earning some money on a temporary job, much to the displeasure of my Morris dancing Headteacher – these conclude my schoolday memories.

11. Joye's Saga

Joye Beckett

I was born in Tranmere, Berken'ead, y'know, the uther side of the wahter from Liverpool … so my ferst school was Mersey Park Infants. I was bi-lingual (Scouse and North-of-Watford middle class) from birth, being allowed to play in the street from an early age.

My first school memory is a vision of a huge blackboard with the words "the" and "and" written in foot high letters, and a class of 50 five year olds chanting "t-h-e the, a-n-d and" over and over again. Enlightened in some ways, our class was sometimes taken into the playground last thing on summer afternoons, where we sat in a huge semi-circle on the little curved-topped brick walls which contained the play area and protected the grimy shrubs beyond.

"Now, who'd like to come and say a poem for us?" Baa baa black sheep ad nauseam! "Anybody else? Something different, perhaps?"

I put up a tentative hand and went out to the front.

"Deep sleeps the winter, cold and wet and grey
Surely all the world is dead, Spring is far away.
But wait! The world shall waken!
It is not dead, for Lo!
The fair maids of February stand in the snow!"

Emboldened by the gushing enthusiasm of the teacher and the "big clap" accorded by my peers, I volunteered the entire contents of 'Flower Fairies of the Spring' – I knew every one by heart! It felt like stardom.

On Empire Day, May 24th, Queen Victoria's birthday, we had a half day holiday, and all morning we played games in the playground and did our drill so smartly and quite perfectly because we were doing it for the Old Queen, and the present distinguished noble King, and for the Empire of which we were so utterly proud. Round and round the playground we ran, our dear little (free!) Union Jacks flying high over our excited noisy heads. Oh, the blissful release rushing about screaming one's head off brings.

But where is the glory now?

Miss Thomas was our Headmistress, little and dumpy as Queen Victoria, and just as authoritarian. She had a cane. It was long and white and

tapering to a fine point, and supple to a ludicrous degree for its purpose.
(She was a kind woman in her way). I suffered its administrations several
times on my palms, mostly for disobedience, (rarely deliberate) and leading
my 'gang' astray, (with every good intention).

The minimal discomfort of this punishment did not prepare me for the
rigours of the Junior School, where the Headmaster had a real, rigid,
vicious cane with a 'knot' two inches from the end which hurt. I can still see
and feel the hot red weals across my left palm. Not the right – no excuse
not to get on with your work. No-one was ever left-handed in our school.
Several children did stammer, though. Miss Taylor, in first year, used to
make us stand in a long line round the edge of the classroom spelling words
in turn, a cane ready in her hand for correcting any mistakes. If a word had
two spellings, you had to say 'which...?' and were told. The child next door
to me was given Bread (or of course Bred). He began: "B...R..." the cane
slashed his hand. The next child to me was asked to spell it. – "B...B..."
again, the cane. There must be two ways of spelling bread! It was my turn.

"Wh...wh... which bread?" I stammered.

"The bread you eat!" Phew!

"B.R.E.A.D." I could spell that.

"Good girl! There'd have been T.R.O.U.B.L.E. with a big capital T if you
hadn't!

I had to ask Mummy what the other "bred" was.

I failed the 11+. In my own defence I must say it could have been because
I had Miss Tickel for the last *two* of my primary years. She took against me
because of my stubborn determination to be my own person, and my refusal
to conform. I couldn't be the goody goody little parson's daughter they all
expected me to be.

The feeling was mutual. I hated her, too. She would ask me a question,
yank me out to the front of the class, ask it again, and yell *"It's obvious!"* in
my face and go all red like a turkey cock. I knew the answer perfectly well
but I wasn't going to tell *her*.

I was the leader of the bad gang in the playground, and Hazel
Braithwaite was the leader of the good gang. Teacher's pets, the lot of them.
They existed mainly to tell-tale on our exploits. When we had to queue up
to have our sewing seen to in needlework, we one day plotted a seriously
good plan. They dared me to carry it out. Miss Tickel had a huge bun low
on the nape of her neck, secured by enormous tortoise-shell hair pins
sticking out all over it. It was the work of seconds to sidle along the queue,
thread a long cotton through a hairpin and sidle back. Phew! No-one in the
Braithwaite gang had seen me. Pause for a while, then gently pull. Ever so
gently. As it came loose, you had to let go of one end of the cotton quickly

and remove the evidence. We never pulled it right out. She absent mindedly pushed it back and she never twigged.

One up to us.

She was away for a fortnight once and we had a beautiful golden-haired young supply teacher, who taught us decimals. I've always been able to do decimals. Funny, that.

When my parents were in Africa and I lived with Aunties and Grandma, I had to walk to and from school four times a day (no-one had dinner at school) and had to cross three main roads, the middle one a five ways junction. It was one and a half miles. No-one thought it too much to ask of an eight year old, least of all me. When my father came home on furlough from Nigeria and his missionary work, he was once asked to come and talk to us all in the school hall about the little black boys and girls'. He called it 'Topsy Turvey land', where children got white-dirty playing on the dusty paths, and in the language they spoke, two phrases could be exactly the same but the way you said them made them entirely different. He illustrated this with the English phrase "Good for nothing" meaning useless and being "Good – for nothing" as asking no reward. Quite a little sermon really. I wonder if any of the other children remember it as I do nearly 70 years on. I doubt it. I basked in reflected glory for days and quite got over the agonising embarrassment I had felt in anticipation.

When we left Mersey Park, everyone went round asking for teacher's autographs, so I did too. In my book Miss Tickel wrote:

"Be good, sweet maid, and let who will be clever
Do noble things, not dream them all day long,
And so make life, death and that vast Forever
One glad sweet song."

Perhaps there was some good in her.

I didn't get my scholarship to Higher Tranmere High School for Girls, but my father paid the three guineas a term for me to join my sister there. She'd been since she was six as she had proved to be too delicate to endure the rough and tumble of Mersey Park. She had every childhood ailment there was, very badly, and broke her leg being run down by a bicycle on Church Road when crossing with her ice cream. She wasn't a brilliant pupil by any means but she was a GOOD GIRL. My main memory of the school is not living up to my sister's goodness.

I was once told to report to my form mistress for 'rank disobedience' because I'd been spotted by Miss Jenkinson (French and Hygiene) without my velour be-ribboned hat on, on the way home from school. I wrote my name and my fault in the Report book, adding 'rank disobedience' because that's what she'd *said!* I got another report for gross impertinence that meant a detention. I had to sit for half an hour after school, writing 'I must not be rude and disobedient' 500 times, gazing intermittently at 'When did you last see your father?' on the detention classroom wall. I got to know that picture very well.

I wasn't a brilliant pupil either, really, and all my inventiveness and imagination seemed to please no-one and was thoroughly squashed. I discovered one thing I could do though. I was told to recite my homework speech from 'Merchant of Venice' one day, and did such justice to 'How sweet the moonlight sleeps upon this bank' that Miss Creswell, (English and Deportment) was moved to give unstinting praise. To *me!* Here was fame indeed. I had the class in hysterics the following year when we were doing 'Little Plays from Shakespeare' and I played Sir Toby Belch in 'The Tricking of Malvolio' from Twelfth Night. (It was an all girls school!) My "Bolts and Shackles!" was brilliant.

Once a week we had to do a thing called Gym. This strange exercise consisted of climbing up impossible ropes, up ladder like walls to dizzying heights; balancing on high precarious bars, hanging upside-down in hoops and – biggest horror of all – struggling to vault over impossibly long and high 'horses'. It was my Achilles' heel. I wasn't alone, of course. One of the other girls got away with being sent home on Gym day because she felt sick. "You weren't sick at all, were you?" accused her mother. "Yes I was" she answered. "I was sick of Gym!!" I longed to be good, or at least adequate at Gym and games, but try as I might, I could not force my springless body over any vaulting horse, and if I managed a somersault I was giddy for a week.

So when it came to Sports Day I wanted to die. If they'd just let me stand on the touch lines and yell "Egg-Green-Egg!" to my team I'd have been a great success, but one had to 'take part'. Not being picked for any hockey or netball team, or athletic race, I was entered for the hundred yards and the sack race!

A grand sports field was hired for the Great Day complete with spectators stand. This was a great wooden tier of seats on the front and steep steps down the back where all the equipment was. We had four houses, named after Scott novels. I was in Woodstock, very proud of the fact that Aileen Little, the glorious slim athletic golden-haired Head Girl of the school was in Woodstock too. How I longed to be like her, how I admired and adored her (from afar!) and would have done almost anything to please her. Except run in a stupid sack race and bring disgrace on Woodstock.

So I hid.

I hid among the sacks and cricket pads and sweaters and hoops and stuff behind the spectators. Imagine me, short, plump and dumpy, with mousy hair, terrified, hearing and ignoring the repetition of my name being called far away, and the towering figure in shorts and Aertex shirt, golden hair neatly pleated back, of Aileen Little the Great appearing menacingly above the top step, looking down at me. "Pritchard! You are in this race. Come ON!"

Those could have been the last words I heard on earth. The mountain of misery and torment I had climbed suddenly led to a precipice of humiliation. My brain shut off. I remember no more!

The school was housed in two great Victorian houses opposite each other in a quiet road, tree lined almost exactly half way between my two childhood homes in Prenton and Tranmere. I never understood why Tranmere Rovers football ground was just across the road from my Prenton (Aunty's) home. Grown ups are so inconsistent.

Otherwise, why should a shop with A. BAKER over the window be a ladies dress shop? It was as well we left Birkenhead in 1936 as the High School was blown up by a land mine in the 1940 Blitz which would have been my final year.

Instead, I went to Ossett Grammer School in the West Riding of Yorkshire, a forward looking, vital, interesting school, but above all, Co-educational! I was put in VLp – Five Lower professional, as opposed to VLc in the commercial stream breeding business men and their secretaries.

I hated changing schools (I hated changing anything!) but once I got there it was all so much more fun than the High School. It was another lovely old Victorian house, but almost a Stately Home with modern corridors leading from it down to a huge gym and assembly hall block, with Domestic Science rooms, and Art Rooms. The Chemy lab was in the stables, and we were surrounded by playing fields and acres of green countryside, only slightly interrupted by a woollen mill where you'd expect a farm.

They couldn't redeem my Maths which had sunk without trace, but here I was set free to be the divergent thinker I was inside. I glowed with the encouragement I got from N.T. Carrington (English and Careers) on my English. Lit *and* lang! (He never got over teaching someone who *liked* parsing, paraphrasing and sentence analysis). I scored in History because we did the same period over again that I'd done at the High School. I caught up quickly in German which they'd been doing for three years, and I blossomed in the Sciences as we hadn't done any in the High School and I arrived just in time to do the last two year School Certificate courses in Biology, Physics and Chemistry. All those experiments and the delicious logic of things. Pussy Parsons taught me Physics with such gentle determination and I passed with credit! Mr Akehurst's Biology and Chemistry lessons were often more philosophical than scientific. I used to go home and argue his opinions with my father, then argue Daddy's back to him. I learnt a lot about people – and life.

When war was declared, the school governors had air raid shelters dug out and built in the school grounds and provided us with hurricane lamps. As there were no other shelters at all in Ossett or its surroundings, the powers that were ordained that we should stay at school throughout the holidays, to be near them in case. We didn't have to work. We, in fact the Upper VIth Science, had done our HSC, and we were due to leave, so Mr Akehurst decided to do a potted photography course in the Chemy lab. All our own Box Brownie shooting, developing, printing and enlarging, and all the chemistry and physics that went with it. I still have my collection of those photographs. Halcyon Days.

Only spoilt by the fact that I failed HSC because I couldn't do the Maths necessary for Physics, and only just passed Chemistry. I got my Distinction in Biology, but that alone did not give me a place at Sheffield University to read Zoology.

So the world got a Nursery and Infant Teacher instead, but that's another story.

12. MOUSE PIE FOR BREAKFAST

Joan Taylor

School memories are mainly of dusty wooden floors, chilblains, Chapel on Sundays, lumpy porridge, "mouse" pie for breakfast and a wire haired terrier called Scruffy, who played a big part in the romance in my life!

I started school when I was 6½ years old. I had learned to read and write at home as I was 4/5 in the family. My first teacher was called Miss Appleton. She was very kind and loving to her children. I was a fluent reader, and so every Friday afternoon, I read to the class whilst Miss Appleton sorted out her percentages in the register. On our birthday, we were allowed to stand on the platform with the teachers, and choose a hymn! I chose 'Jerusalem', which seems a strange choice now, but my mother would often sing it as she worked in the house.

When I was eight years old, my father died. He had been ill for a year, and so there was no money left. My sister and I were sent away to a school called The Royal Orphanage. My father had been a Freemason and his friends managed to secure places for us. The next seven years of my life leave me with very mixed memories. On a cold January day, we left our loving family and warm and cosy house to enter this Institution. We lived by the clock. Every minute of every day was organised for us. Each morning we rose at 7 a.m. and after dressing, had to run two laps round the front drive of the school, about ¾ mile in all. The weather made no difference, pity the poor teacher who had to stand at the end of the drive ticking our numbers off in her book! The boys hung out of their windows making 'yah boo' noises at us! Breakfast often consisted of very lumpy porridge (no sugar or milk) – every lump had to be eaten; or perhaps 'Mouse' Pie (a concoction of left over vegetables and meat baked in a tin in the oven until crisp and hard.) After breakfast we did our chores according to the roster – washing up (the worst job – no Fairy Liquid), cleaning out the dormitories, ironing in the laundry (lovely in winter because the old flat irons warmed our frozen mitts), or polishing shoes.

School lessons started at 9 a.m. and lasted until 12.30 when we had time to wash and line up for dinner. The milk puddings made this meal memorable, because they were ladled out on to tea plates at 11 a.m. and so were set solid by dinner time. The game was to hold the plate upside down and see whose pudding fell off first. All food served had to be consumed, so often we transferred the worst bits to the pockets in our knickers, to be dealt with later. If you were unfortunate enough to be caught by the teacher on duty, you were put on a diet of the particular food for a week! I remember a girl called Gwen living on cabbage for a week! We sat on benches for meals and were not allowed to let our backs sag.

I enjoyed lessons, they seemed interesting and stopped you feeling sad or hungry, and we had lots of what is called Preparation to do. After tea each evening, all the screens were folded back between the classrooms and we all settled down to homework. The youngest ones did ½ hour, the next group 1 hour and the seniors 1¾ hours.

I enjoyed English, Maths especially Algebra and Geometry, Scripture but French was a disaster lesson. The French teacher had an explosive temper, and would often hurl the whole set of exercise books at the head of some poor soul who had a D mark! I was often the recipient! Art and needlework were a trial, but the teacher for these subjects was pleasant. The work at the school was considered to be of a high standard and we all took Cambridge School Certificates and passed. Sundays were devoted to Chapel, silence and walks. It started with 8 a.m. chapel service for communicants, then breakfast, then silence in class until 10.30 a.m. when we got dressed for Chapel. Matins was at 11 a.m. and this was when we got a chance to see the boys. There was a Boys School but we were not supposed to talk to them. On Sunday evenings brothers were allowed to meet their sisters for 30 minutes. Many notes were exchanged between boys and girls at this meeting.

After matins, the girls went for a walk in crocodile for about 30 minutes, then we had a little time to ourselves before Sunday dinner. After this meal (knicker pockets full of cabbage) we all sat in silence and wrote a letter home. These letters were all censored by the Headmistress before being posted, so it was no good complaining, it would only mean that your mother didn't get a letter and so would be worried about you. After letter writing, at 2.30 we set out for our afternoon walk. This lasted between one hour and two, depending on the age and fitness of the poor teacher, who had to accompany this crocodile of 120 girls. When we got back, all of our shoes had to be taken off and one 'house' of girls would be detailed to clean them all. Insteps had to be blackened as well as the uppers.

The next meal was tea, 2 slices of bread and marg and a piece of cake, in the week we had bread and jam, or bread and black treacle.

Evensong was 6.30 p.m. I loved this service. In winter the Chapel was very warm and comforting after a long miserable day, and of course we had the boys to look over.

When we got home from Chapel we had FREE time till we went to bed at 7.30 or 8.30 according to our age.

I was very bad at Sport and would rather not remember the awful Hockey Matches with skinned ankles and freezing hands, so no more about that. Now the Boys School was quite separate from the Girls School. We each had our own Head, but in 1934 a revolution took place, when it was announced that the Senior Boys and Senior Girls would attend a Christmas Dance. This was to be a Fancy Dress Dance. I don't know where we found the things from, but we did dress up and I went as a Pirate. We wore our bedroom slippers, as our heavy shoes would have scratched the Oak Floor. There was much practising before hand. My first partner was a chap called 'Plum' Taylor. We danced together every dance, but kept getting parted by the Head, who thought this was not quite correct.

He asked me if I would smile at him in Chapel on Sunday. He explained that he sat in the back row of the choir (he had a lovely baritone voice), and so began our romance. I was just eleven years old. Plum wrote in his diary that night "Tonight I have met the girl I am going marry". Ten years later he did that, and showed me that diary.

Sunday evenings became a very important time for me, because when I was a Senior Prefect, one of my jobs was to take that little wirehaired scruffy terrier for a walk before I went to bed. The dog always seemed to want to run up the back of the chapel and of course I had to catch him. Strangely enough there was usually someone to meet me.

The independence and discipline I learned at this school has stood me in good stead all my life. The school is now independent and co-educational as the need for this kind of institution is no more, thanks to the Welfare State.

13. FIRST DAYS

Patricia Morton

The long Summer holiday had seemed to stretch unending. Changing schools had added an extra week to mine and it seemed that commencement day would never come. But at last came the morning and I was early away, down the suburban road and through the deserted park over the cool damp grass. Hurrying, because there was a train to catch, which was exciting and novel and then onwards to find the correct bus.

Novel also was the smart uniform, regulation heavy wool navy blazer, velour hat, badged and banded with bright school colours over a box pleated, square necked tunic and long thick black stockings. It would be a warm afternoon journey home!

Today was to be the day of the Book List purchases. Shepherded and supervised by our new form mistresses, we would go to buy second-hand text books from the girls who had preceded us the previous year. Prices were minimal, one and fourpence for example, for one in reasonable condition and some even cheaper. We were required to put on fresh covers for of course some would be resaleable next year. Girls were requested not to put their names inside in ink – but I recall using some bearing three or four inscriptions. At the time, I pondered on these, thinking the originators to be very old, possibly even at least fourteen by then! Some new text books also were always needed, and the delight in opening publications such as a brightly coloured atlas with its distinctive smell of printers' inks has remained until today. Even the more severe black and white print became more inviting.

Great care was taken in putting the new possessions tidily in one's own single desk, (an attitude which didn't last!) and we could begin to feel we belonged.

The school buildings seemed vast, though warm and pleasant, although the general layout remained a mystery for quite a while. Certain lessons required us to go elsewhere and woe betide the one who omitted to gather up everything required for the move. Our form room was away up on the second floor in what seemed to us a remote corner indeed. One could get lost if the rest of the group went too far ahead, and then get into hot water for lateness at the next lesson. Despite these minor traumas I was impressed by the interior of the buildings. Much polished oak, gold lettered Honours Boards in the main hall, a new gymnasium and a large laboratory with its own peculiar odours assailing the nose as one went in.

On reflection, we were beginning to integrate quite quickly, coming to terms with the multiplicity of subjects and Staff, whose own varying expectations demanded diverse and positive reactions on our part, new disciplines both inside school and out. The girls' behaviour was monitored also outside school hours and reports of cardinal sins such as going home without the school hat on, brought down inevitable wrath on meekly bent heads.

As a sample cross section of the then current society, my new class mates could hardly be bettered. Parental origins and occupations varied across the social strata from professionals to craftsmen, designers to industrial workers and by no means all city born and bred. Children from Scottish, Irish, half-French and Italian families joined the local born, some travelling from surrounding counties, and from a primary education equally varied, all to blend in the magic mix of school discipline and navy blue uniforms.

One morning during the first term I was late starting out to catch the train. By now there was a much heavier satchel to carry, but nevertheless I raced through the rain sodden park towards the station. Steam was pulsing into the sky as I reached the top of the greasy black steps only to see the green flag waving and hear the great engine shrug into action. I was too late! What now? Miserably I turned back, tears brimming, heading for the station steps. Suddenly there was a hand on my shoulder and I heard a voice – "Come along little miss, be quick! Look! He's waiting for you!" The monster had halted – sizzling and spitting its opinion of late comers! Someone opened a carriage door and hauled me inside smiling as the great wheels began revolving again in response to the powerful steam engine.

After that, I sampled other routes and methods of travelling. Trams were more plentiful than trains, squealing and swaying along the middle of the roads, and cyclists were none too pleased when front wheels occasionally jammed in the tramlines. A few open topped, yellow buses were still in use with outside stairs to the upper deck. I enjoyed watching homegoing schoolboys who used to dare each other to jump the steps from top to bottom holding the rail with one hand, to the great wrath of the bus conductor. All to no avail because they were off and away out of reach laughing as they ran.

Soon to most of us it seemed that the days of the primary school were long gone. The great amalgamation had begun. Pride grew in the school teams, school achievements, our own developing skills opening out new vistas. Gradually one became a part of all this, absorbed into an ongoing system which became our school world until the next great upheaval in our lives, when we left armed with a philosophy to stand us in good stead for the years to come.

Young children starting school in the twenties.

By the time this little boy was photographed, probably one in ten families owned a Kodak or Brownie easy-to-use box camera. Colour film came a few years later in 1935.

Airship R101 attracted nationwide interest. Maiden flight October 1929 crashed in France in 1930 on an inaugural flight to India.

A 'progressive' infant classroom arrangement for the period. Rows of
wooden 'twin' desks were more usual. Note the individual work trays,
the wendy house and the sand tray with models.

A car for the larger family of the day. Henry Ford's pioneer
engineering mass-production methods turned out over one million
cars annually with costs halved. At last his dream of a people's
car came true. Ford's methods boosted industry worldwide.

St. James School – Standard 6.

1926

*The British brand of family runabout.
'Baby Austin' Seven and 'Bullnose' Morris
Cowley production boomed. Soon these
could be bought for £25 down then £2 per
week.*

*Schoolboy
1930s.
Preparatory
School
uniform.*

The Great Hall and Chamberlain Clock Tower. Granted a Royal Charter in 1900, the University was formally opened by King Edward the Seventh in 1909. Joseph Chamberlain became its first Chancellor.

The General Strike. A London Bus, with volunteer driver and police escort sitting on the bonnet.

Many city dwellers valued their small gardens and created oases of colour for their family's enjoyment.

1932

RADIO ENTERS ITS GOLDEN YEARS

From new headquarters, Britain's broadcasting service widened the appeal of 'wireless' by adding fun to the facts

Motto
'Educate, Inform, Entertain'

Ten years on, now a Corporation by Royal Charter with two regular daily programmes entitled the National and Regional.

What would it be like away from home? Major cities were expected to become immediate targets at the outbreak of World War Two. Teachers and pupils were rapidly evacuated to country homes.

Winston Churchill's 'V for Victory'

Strict food rationing and restriction of imports meant that children of this little girl's age would not taste bananas until World War Two was over. Because clothing coupons could not stretch to provide regulation school uniform, rules were relaxed on the wearing of white blouses, school colours and such.

The latest model – about 1918.

14. IRISH SCHOOLDAYS

Peggy McIntyre

My only memory of my first school – a Convent where I spent a year – is of a big house in its own grounds. I certainly did not learn to read or write there (in English) since I remember one of my brothers teaching me to write my name to enable me to join the library when I was six years old. I cannot work out how I learned to read in English. I did not study it as a subject until my fourth year in Scoil Bhride (St. Bridget's School); possibly a brother taught me.

My last two years at school were again at a large Convent School – Irish speaking, of course. For me it was like a Sixth Form College. Life was serious when aged 16-18 preparing for Leaving Certificate – 'A' level equivalent – there was, however, no specialisation, all subjects were taken in the examination. I was not involved in any extra curricular activities there and remember only one enlightened teacher (lay) who taught us Latin and Irish, not just for the forthcoming exams but as a part of one's education.

I was educated at Scoil Bhride where I spent ten years from age 6–16, a type of primary school I suppose, except that one could stay on to take the Intermediate Certificate ('O' levels). It was state subsidised but also had an affiliation with the nearby University – post graduate teachers occasionally took classes.

It was an "All Irish" School – all subjects taught in Irish and Irish only spoken in school – we were on our honour not to speak English in school and dutifully abided by that ruling. All text books were in Irish, especially in the earlier years.

I have never questioned until now why I was sent there. It was a strange choice inasmuch as my background was not in any way Political/ Nationalist; none of my family knew or spoke Irish. Perhaps my widowed mother heard that it was a good school, or more likely she was impressed by the fact that it was free. My father died when I was an infant and there were five of us, the others all several years older than I was.

I walked to school (alone) as I had in my previous school until I got a bicycle when aged 10. It was about half a mile from home and quite near the City Centre though it did not seem so in those days. The building was a typical Dublin Georgian terraced house. I can remember white carved marble fireplaces in some of the rooms but then most of us lived in similar houses. It was four stories high with narrow winding stairs up to the top classes; the heating was open coal fires – no fire regulations in those days. The playground was a long cemented suburban garden with an extra classroom built at the end where the stables would have been, with a bicycle shed and the back gate opening on to a lane – our entrance to school. The basement had been cleared into a large open area, I remember large concrete supports. There were cloakrooms along the side and a row of washbasins – the lavatories were outside.

School hours were from 9-3 with a half hour break for lunch – bread and jam, nothing as sophisticated as sandwiches, and a bottle of milk in a medicine bottle probably, drunk directly from the container – sounds Dickensian but there had been porridge and a cooked breakfast before setting out for school and dinner always at 3.30 on return from school. On wet days we were allowed to spend the break in the basement – otherwise we were herded out into the yard. In the classroom there were desks for two with ink wells, and a filthy job it was to be put in charge of filling the inkwells, as well as blackening the blackboards weekly – we had to do these chores in turn. In the higher classes we were assigned to running the school

libraries – cupboards of books, one for religious books, one for fiction. The latter stocked with books which most of us donated on leaving school – I remember I gave "The Prisoner of Zenda". There were probably other tasks which I do not remember, there was always a particular emphasis on duty and responsibility.

Holidays were about eight weeks duration in summer with 3–4 weeks at Christmas and Easter, no half term breaks or Saturday school. I fiercely resented having to go to school on Saturday mornings in my last two years at school, mostly for improving lectures from visiting ecclesiastics. Subjects taught in the first four years were I suppose the 3 Rs in Irish. Thereafter, History (mainly Irish with a treasury of Irish Mythology), Geography, English, French (the Headmistress grew up in France), Irish (taught by a native speaker, I think from the Aran Islands) and Maths. We did Latin for one year only in one of the higher classes; I think we all had to pay a small sum for the outside tutor employed. Classes in the early years were probably large (boys were admitted up to age 8), about 30 pupils per class, but became progressively smaller in the higher classes, the most affluent, upwardly mobile, peeling off to prestigious Convent schools. I remember in my last year there were only about ten of us, a happy arrangement, though I think that only three of us went to University, life in the thirties was harsh for many. My family was by no means affluent but I went to the theatre occasionally and of course to "the pictures", the dream palace of the thirties, and there was the library. God bless Andrew Carnegie – I do not care if he made his money from munitions – did he? – he opened magic casements for many of my generation.

I do not remember any punishments such as detention at Scoil Bhride; to be summoned to the Headmistress's study was a powerful deterrent. She was an outstanding woman dedicated and enlightened, fair and just.

There was a system of stars for achievement, not necessarily academic but for conduct also; each pupil belonged to a group – there were four I think with distinguishing sashes and badges which had to be earned. Each term the highest "achievers" in each group were given a party, paid for I suspect by the headmistress – gooey shop cakes. Annually the creme de la creme were taken on an outing. I managed it once: we were taken to the seaside, tea in a restaurant, followed by a visit to the funfair – rides on the dodgems, bliss. On the feast of St. Bridget there were two parties at the school, an early one for the juniors, later for the older pupils, games and again luscious SHOP cakes!

We were taken from school to the theatre, Shakespeare usually at The Gate, strangely never to the national theatre, the Abbey, the productions there were maybe controversial at the time – I do not know. Another surprising thing, on reflection, is that we were never in any way indoctrinated politically. I suppose this is understandable, the Civil War was a recent memory to all the older people. We were made aware of our cultural heritage and taught our history endlessly up to 1900 but not after then.

We were encouraged to compete in the Feiseann – inter-school competitions, Irish poetry recitations, conversation, etc. We also put on plays at the Mansion House, again inter-school competitions, and taken there to concerts from the Number One Army Band. The greatest 'value' from the point of view of we lucky few was broadcasting. The station was called 2RN – a pokey studio on the top floor of the General Post Office. We broadcast plays etc. for the Children's Hour – all in a day's work but were taken to tea afterwards in a restaurant on the proceeds. These proceeds in my time also bought a radio for the school.

Scoil Bhride for me was a most happy place. I made good friends, with one of whom I am still in touch, and a couple of others I meet now and then. I learned more than half of "The Golden Treasury" off by heart, even Gerard Manley Hopkins, not easy to memorise. We were doing Shakespeare when about 10 years old, an English reader I remember very early on was "Cranford". The Headmistress inculcated my joy in English literature, though my mother was forever spouting poetry.

Miss Gavan Duffy had I believe a vision of an educated, responsible, disciplined individual and to the best of her ability and the material available, strove to mould us into her ideal form. I was indeed fortunate to have been sent to her school.

NORTHERN IRELAND

A newspaper cutting showing Belfast schoolgirls prepared for possible trials of war against Adolf Hitler in 1939.

Students at Victoria College, Belfast.

15. A Bit of (Religious) Education

Cora Jacobs

It was at a meeting of parents of one of our Jewish youth organisations that I happened to mention the name "Pizer's" and the lack of response around the table indicated, if I didn't realise already, that I was older than anyone else there and that my memories of that establishment went back – heavens! – over sixty years.

Upon retiring from the headmastership of the Hebrew school, where according to my father he had supervised the education of *his* generation in the no-nonsense fashion of the day, when a clip on the ear produced results of a kind, Mr. Pizer had set up his part-time school of religious education in his home in Pershore Road, and on Saturday afternoons, Sunday mornings and Tuesday evenings my sisters, brothers and myself were compulsory pupils.

The younger children were taught in Mrs. Pizer's dining room, where the faint aroma of the Sabbath meal seemed always present, and our studies were supervised by earnest, kindly Mrs. Katie Levy, who taught us our Aleph Beits and told us Bible stories. When we were considered sufficiently prepared we climbed the stairs to the top of the house where the old gentleman himself taught in a tiny attic room almost filled by an oblong deal table with just room for the boys to sit round three sides and the few girl pupils on the outer edge. I remember also there was a blackboard behind the door, on an easel.

I was a timid child, and my first climb up that staircase was made more fearful by the dark hints of awfulness thrown out by my teasing older sisters. I soon discovered to my relief that most of our greybearded mentor's severities were reserved for the boys, especially the bigger ones whom he frequently addressed as "mishpot" – rubbish heap – and when particularly infuriated by their stupidity he would land out at the nearest head at the end of the row, who would then fall with exaggerated agony onto his neighbour, causing the whole class to collapse sidewards and require some time to regain equilibrium. We girls did not entirely escape his attention, however, and one of his favourite means of obtaining ours was a pinch of the cheek between horny finger and thumb and the warning "I won't marry you when you grow up, my dear". He was to me the incarnation of Fagin, poor old man.

The tiny window overlooked the County Cricket Ground and on Saturday afternoons in summer, if he had cause to leave the room for a few minutes, there would be a rush for this window by the boys and an even greater traffic jam as soon as his step was heard returning. Any luckless lad who had not succeeded in regaining his place was 'in for it'.

When class was over, the boy or boys whose Barmitzvah year it was, would stay behind for extra tuition – there were some advantages in being born female, after all!

As time passed I discovered, almost against my will, that Hebrew was becoming a little more comprehensible, and the day arrived when some elementary grammar actually engaged my interest, but shortly afterwards my attendance at the house in Pershore Road was abruptly ended as family finances plunged into the doldrums and economies became necessary. I was sorry, though, when I heard that the old man had died.

16. Education in the London Style

Ron Levy

The School Board for London built sturdily. Each Elementary School had three storeys. The lowest was for the Infants, the middle one for the Boys and the top for the Girls who also enjoyed a roof playground. Even before the Muslim influence, boys and girls were strictly separated. The classrooms were arranged around the hall and were all of glass, so that the Head teacher sitting in his or her desk in the hall (there was no office in those days) could see what was going on in every classroom, and could burst in upon a lesson and say "Mr......., there is a boy talking in your class".

In retrospect I am amazed at the extraordinary quality of the teachers. In those days the only way a poor person could enter higher education was to opt for teaching with all expenses paid. Hence the ablest and most intelligent of the working classes found their way into the profession. Classes were on the average about sixty. The registers contained spaces for 65. Perhaps, as a consequence of this, caning was endemic. It was done, as I recall, without malice. Talking in class, bad or untidy work would inevitably bring down the cane. Often boys would deliberately misbehave, if the lessons became too boring, in order to provide a welcome distraction. If you were not caned at least two or three times a week, you were considered a "cissy", and so you would provide a certain reaction. I remember my Uncle Barney – a sweet, gentle, scholarly man who faced these barbaric conditions all his working life, was horrified to learn that I was to go into teaching. He begged my mother to make me an Estate Agent. His own children went to Cambridge and Oxford on scholarships and became very successful lawyers.

Learning was by rote. Every morning after statutory prayers, the whole school would recite all the multiplication tables up to 12, and then all the pre-decimalisation weights and measures. I was long puzzled by what sounded like "Fiveenarf yaya one rodpole or perch".

Although Catholics and Jews didn't go into prayers but stayed in the classroom, I quickly learnt all the hymns, but found the Lord's Prayer completely incomprehensible. In broad Cockney it came over as "Ow far we

chart inem 'Hallo' by thy name". An imaginative child, I saw a kind of navigation exercise looking for the abode of angels. Another source of perplexity was the hymn "There is a Green Hill far away without a City Wall". I wondered why on earth a green hill far away should ever feel the need for a city wall. Tables, prayers and hymns were all recited in the same monotonous sing-song tone.

Beside the cane, another relief from boredom would be putting your hand up and ask "to be excused". Toilets were outside and you could take plenty of time getting there and back. Staff also used the outside toilets, but had a special cubicle, kept locked. The key was held by the teacher of Standard III and boys would be sent by their teacher from another class to ask for the key. This particular teacher was very toilet-conscious. At play-time he would follow the boys into the loo to make sure they performed, and did not have to be excused during lessons. I can remember with what triumph he once told us how a boy said he didn't want to go, but when the teacher stood behind him he produced an enormous stream!

Dinner time was between 12 noon and 2 p.m. We all used to go home for our dinner, but the ragged boys had a mysterious repast called "lunch". At morning playtimes their mothers would stand behind the locked gates of the playground and hand them packets of sandwiches. They contained, so I was told, mostly bread and dripping or bread and sugar.

It was an orderly, disciplined world. Children felt secure and knew exactly where they stood. Right was very clearly distinguished from wrong, and wrong was inevitably punished. Right was rewarded by good conduct marks and scholarships to secondary schools. Happy days!

17. VERY EARLY TIMES AND NOT SO EARLY TIMES

Bert Sargent

I was born on November 23rd 1917 at 11 Fern Bank, Grant Street, Edgbaston, Birmingham, and christened Albert Arthur after my father and my father's brother, who was killed in World War I at the age of 17. In all honesty these are not my favourite names. I was known as Bert to differentiate from my father who was called Albert. The only time I received my full name was from my mother on official occasions or when I had done wrong. In recent years I have responded to Bertie – not that I am greatly enamoured of this diminutive either. Most of my working life I was known as Sarge.

Our house was nearest to town. Shopping trips by relations usually ended up at our house with cups of tea and cakes, mostly my mother's side of the family, plus Aunt Liz my father's youngest sister.

Aunts Kate and Martha were the most frequent callers. Aunt Martha used to come every Thursday afternoon. For some reason she did Gran's washing. How this came about I do not know. Aunt Kate arrived one Saturday afternoon, marched through the back door, and sat on the chair just inside, saying as she did so 'Bill Bailey's come home'. My father had removed the seat for repair and she was well and truly stuck. Her language on this stressful occasion was choice.

The time was fast approaching when I would have to start school as I would be 5 in November. Just before Christmas mother stayed in bed and the doctor and a lady arrived. Some time later I was asked if I would like to see my baby brother who was to be called Robert Eric. After that bit of excitement I started school at St. Thomas's, Granville Street. One day on the way to school, clutching my mother's hand, I slipped and fell, hitting my head on the kerbstone and a large lump appeared in no time. Whether because of this accident or not I became ill and was away from school for several months. I never returned to St. Thomas's but went to St. James' School in Summer Road. The juniors' hours were 9–12 and 2–4. There were no school meals but we had a third of a pint of milk a day.

Friday afternoon's last session was my favourite. Miss ·Smith, our teacher, would read stories. I used to feel sorry for her because she always had a big bottle of asprins on her desk which I thought meant she had a permanent headache – maybe she had with us to contend with!

My best friend was Norman Allbut who lived in Summer Road, quite near the school, and my other friend was Bernard Callaghan who lived in Lee Bank Road.

Mr. Millard was the Headmaster. He travelled to and from school on a Martinside motor bike and sidecar, a very rare machine since only a handful were made. Today it would be worth a fortune. He was very keen on music and trained a choir of the older children to sing descants. Every morning we had assembly and sang a hymn with a descant. On Thursday mornings we walked to St. James' for a short service. This was a High Church with incense and Latin responses.

Mr. Millard started a Scout troop, the 34th Birmingham. Grey shirt and shorts, black neckerchief with red border. I was in Raven Patrol. The Scoutmaster was Mr. Paterson who was trained at Queens College to be an Architect. He had a Hare lip.

Mr. Paterson came from Cheltenham, he arranged a weeks camp for us in the Cotswolds on a Captain Bunbury's estate. Mr. P. made a map of the area and gave us each a blue print copy.

It was a good introduction to the pleasures of camping – it rained nearly all the time. We had to hack out a clearing in the heather before we could put up the tents. Then a latrine had to be dug, a fireplace built, then a table with bench seats and a roof to keep out the rain.

One night the R101 Airship passed overhead with all its cabins ablaze with lights. It was on a trial flight before the disastrous flight to India only reaching France before crashing. I did see it again on the day I came home from camp, it passed over Birmingham in the daylight this time.

Whilst in the Scouts, we competed in a musical, singing camp fire songs trained by Mr. Millard of course. We also took part in a Football Contest. We were runners-up in both events.

The final event that I took part in was a weekend competition camp. We failed miserably, some one spiking our stew with a bar of soap.

Standard 4 was the turning point in your scholastic career when you started extra work for the 11+ examinations for entry to the Grammar Schools. I did the work but when the exams came I was ill and so missed out on the Grammar School. This class was taken by Mr. Parsons who was a strict disciplinarian and had a cane which he used frequently. We all became experts in the art of caning, listening to his little lectures. 'Take a firm grip, and just a short movement of the cane is all that is required'. He was always prepared to give a demonstration if it was not clear! Cissie Peters, a Jewish girl who lived just round the corner from us had many tussles and canings from Mr. Parsons.

If the stress became too hard for her to bear she just went home! I was shy and quiet and my main idea was to get through the school day without causing any ripples – in fact not to be noticed at all. Teachers were strict and only one or two would talk to you 'man to man'.

Standard 5 – Mr. Franklin was young and new to the school. His control of the class was suspect and his temper was vile.

Standard 6 – Miss Craddock, my favourite teacher. I did my best work whilst with her. She talked to us and asked our opinion on things which stimulated interest.

Standard 7 – Mr. Neath, who was also sports master. He had an A.J.S. motor cycle with a square tank. He used to take us to the playing fields which were some distance away along the Pershore Road. First we had to walk to the Bristol Road and catch a special tram. It was quite a ride. We went up the Bristol Road to Pebble Mill Road, down Pebble Mill along Pershore Road to Wallace Road, some distance past Cannon Hill Park. The playing fields were at the bottom of Wallace Road. We would play cricket or soccer, depending on the season. The girls played netball in the summer – what they did in the winter I don't know.

Standard 8 – We had a lady teacher whose name escapes me. She was quite good and I did some of my best work with her. In my last term at school I was top of the class in the exams.

By this time I was 13 years old and had passed the entrance exam to Aston Commercial School, where I duly went.

I had obtained a free place but had to buy all text books. Subjects were Maths, Geography, Book Keeping, Science, French, English, Shorthand, Typing, Mechanical Drawing, P.E. and games. It offered 2 or 3 year courses. In the third year Spanish was added to the 2 year course subjects. The school was in Whitehead Road, Aston, which entailed a cross city trip on bus or tram, change in town. Fortunately a new bus service started which ran from Quinton to Kingstanding via Aston so I could travel all the way without changing. The school catered for girls and boys although they were taught separately for the first two years.

We learnt Gregg shorthand as it was supposed to be quicker than Pitman. We were taught touch typing and typed away merrily to music from an old gramophone fitted with a large horn stuffed with old dusters to cut down the noise. By the end of our time we were supposed to do 80 words a minute shorthand and 60 typing. Our teacher dictated for shorthand in short bursts but in the tests we sometimes got another teacher who would dictate continuously, which caused problems. In addition to academic lessons we had swimming one afternoon per week. I didn't stay for the third year – perhaps as well as I would have started Spanish and had enough trouble with French.

And so ended my school days.

Schooldays Afterthoughts – School Clinic
– A postscript by Bert Sargent

The school nurse used to visit our school at regular intervals. The one visit everyone dreaded was head inspection. This was to check for nits and ringworm. If you had either of these you were sent off to the Clinic where your hair was shaved down to the wood. If I remember correctly, ring worm sufferers had their heads painted with a violet coloured solution.

We had a weekly routine at home – mother would spread a newspaper on the table then we would have to bend over while she combed our hair with a tooth comb. The resultant bits on the newspaper were carefully examined for anything that moved.

Another nurse would examine our teeth. Then our hearing was tested – this was usually done by a teacher who sat at the desk and whispered some instructions. You were seated a set distance away and if you could hear would obey. If not, a visit to the clinic was arranged. I was fortunate, thanks to mother's vigilance, and a family friend who was a dentist and did not have to visit the Clinic.

There was also a free issue of clothing and boots for needy children which was sponsored by The Birmingham Mail Fund.

18. WARTIME SCHOOLING

Ken Morris

D uring the peaceful years from 1932 to 1938 I was at Colmore Rd School. At home we used loose tea from a caddy and it was ages before I understood why the Head was called 'Teabags' instead of Miss Tetley. After six uneventful but happy years, I was summoned one day to the front of Assembly in the hall. As a reward for doing well in the 11+ exam., I could choose the hymn to be sung. Without reference to the gathering war clouds; simply because the tune appealed to a ten year old, the school sang 'Onwards Christian Soldiers, marching as to war.'

A year later, so they were, but in the meantime, school uniform and books had to be bought and six days a week I cycled to the temporary huts that were home to King Edwards School on the Bristol Road, Edgbaston. 'Domine salvum fac regem' was on our blazers and this was to become more than a symbolic prayer for the sovereign, when the Luftwaffe bombed Buckingham Palace.

It didn't take long to learn that the prefects at K.E.S. had the power to cane and that the Headmaster, the Reverend E. T. England, exercised that power. He inflicted a mass flogging of three strokes apiece on all the boys of Shells A and B after a lunchtime fight had resulted in Welch being thrown THROUGH THE CLASSROOM WINDOW!

Just before war broke out, School was evacuated to Repton in Derbyshire and six of us were billeted in a local doctor's squash court alongside his house. On 3rd September 1939, we were called in to listen to Mr. Chamberlain's declaration of war on Germany and to have a Sunday meal. This included meat, which the doctor insisted I must eat although I was (and remain) a vegetarian. Before my mother brought me home from the doctor's dietary regime, I had time to get ceremoniously expelled from the school Scout troop for failing to do the good deed of weeding Repton churchyard.

Back in Kings Heath, schooling consisted of mornings only at Wheelers Lane Senior Boys, until the end of that Autumn term. There I met a lad who had no names at all but answered to any. His anonymity intrigued staff and boys alike. The Spring and Summer terms were spent at Kings Norton Secondary School for Boys on an alternate morning or afternoon

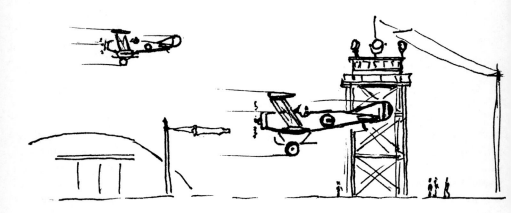

basis with boys from other K.E. Foundation Schools. We fought regular snowball battles against the host school in the early wintry days and we enjoyed cricket matches on their playing field later on. After one such game, a K.E.S. lad with a slight stammer, explained to me that his middle name was Peacock after his father, of Peacock Stores fame, whilst his surname was his mother's. This seemed odd at the time but I was more interested in another boy's assertion that his parents walked around their garden without clothes – he would not say where they lived. I told them I had played football at Highbury with Ted Drake. This was true as the Arsenal Star came to visit his girlfriend in Shutlock Lane, thus emulating the Chamberlains, who had also travelled from Highbury in London to Highbury Park, Birmingham.

Incidentally, Kenneth Peacock Tynan became a theatre critic in later years and more of him anon.

With the Battle of Britain at its height, K.E.S. moved back from Repton in September 1940. The new buildings at Edgbaston had been virtually completed despite the war, and we re-joined our own school in time to listen avidly to the numbers of German 'planes shot down each day.

One sunny afternoon that Autumn Term, when cycling home up Donkey's Hollow to Moor Green Lane, I watched a German 'plane fly low over Kings Heath firing its machine guns. Chipped bricks in a house at the corner of Shutlock Lane still bear witness to this indiscriminate attack. Much worse followed in night raids and two HE (High Explosive) bombs landed in Shutlock Lane near our house. By day we searched Highbury Park for AA gun shrapnel and fire bombs, which were located by black patches left in the turf. Nights were spent in the Anderson Shelter in our back garden. It was cold, damp and dark and not conducive to doing homework especially with a one year old sister in residence. Just after Italian prisoners of war had filled in the craters in the road, another bomb fell in the front garden and demolished the front of our house, No. 26. Mud and rubble fell onto our shelter. We moved down the road to stay with Mr. Stanley, the Air Raid Warden at No. 36, after which we stayed with Grandad at Cannon Hill for a while.

At this time Dad was No.E601 in the Kings Heath Wartime Emergency Police and had been directed to assist his Coventry colleagues during their devastating blitz. For some days we knew nothing of his whereabouts and he came back to find his house bombed and family missing. We were eventually rehoused in a place without electricity but with an indoor Morrison shelter on which we could play table tennis. I did little schooling from then until well into 1941.

By way of contribution to the war effort, my brother and I had run a fuel collection service for ourselves and selected elderly neighbours. We took our trolleys on a regular basis to the Bournville Factory premises by the railway, where Cadbury's piled up unwanted packing cases and timber. We also helped Dad to 'dig for victory' on a splendidly productive allotment off Russell Rd. It had a hut in which we brewed tea, and frequently stayed overnight.

An elderly allotment holder there fascinated us with tales of a Civil War battle which took place on this site by Cannon Hill Park 300 years earlier. He also showed us a clump of trees beneath which were buried the bodies of the slain.

These were probably casualties from a skirmish before the Battle of Edghill in October 1642.

Apart from providing recruits for the armed forces, K.E.S. also did its bit for the war effort on the home front. All boys were enrolled in either the Scouts, the Air Training Corps or the Junior Training Corps (ex O.T.C.) in which we wore khaki uniform with puttees, World War I style and learned to drill and to fire rifles. Farm camps were held each summer at Newnham Bridge, Herefordshire where we helped to weed hops, drink their products, and pick plums. I fell out of one tree and frequently got stung by wasps. We went swimming in the River Teme and learned to play Bridge in the evenings. By the time of the fifth form, I was in the A.T.C. and learned Morse Code, Aldis signalling and Aircraft recognition. Several camps were held at Midland R.A.F. Stations such as Halfpenny Green, and we cadets were given training flights in 'planes such as Ansons, Oxfords and Blenheims – always with a parachute! After promotion to Corporal, I was sent on a course to R.A.F. Cranwell in Lincolnshire and was treated to an exhibition of ancient biplanes flying against a gale. They appeared to be going backwards past the control tower and we were told (correctly) that we should never see such a sight again.

After this exciting experience, came a monotonous spell of war work. Sixth form boys were directed in the long summer vacation to various war factories and I worked for six weeks from 8 a.m. to 6 p.m. at Precision Chasers in Kings Norton Factory Centre tapping screwholes into pieces of brass to be used in bomb fuses. At the time, I cheered announcements of bomber raids into Germany but was desperately bored when helping to provide the means, and never wanted to hear the sound of "Music While You Work" again.

Back at school, Kenneth Peacock Tynan lived up to his middle name with brilliant displays in academic work and in producing plays such as 'Hellsapoppin'. In this extravaganza, at his request, I ran across stage aimlessly in House rugger kit.

When School Dinners seemed less than cordon bleu, some of the older lads walked up to Selly Oak British Restaurant, which provided a good meal for 9d. An additional attraction was the newsagents' en route where 'Health and Efficiency' magazines could be perused. Did these provoke the spectacular display from Tynan when he stood on a table in the British Restaurant one day and harangued the bemused diners on the subject of Free Love? Apart from his being the only boy in our year to win a Scholarship at Oxford, my only other recollection of Tynan was that he served as school bookie, and took weeks to pay out winnings when Hackett romped home in the school mile.

During the war years at school, staff changes were frequent. An elderly clergyman, refugee professors and several lady teachers helped out. With their assistance, I managed to pass the London University Matriculation in 1942, failing however in Physics. In mitigation, the refugee Doctor who taught us, spoke English little better than we spoke Czech and some of us were baffled as he placed pins by mirrors or iron filings by magnets. Higher School Certificate was passed in 1944 in French, German and Spanish, but I gained an unusual distinction by failing in English.

A final recollection of schooldays was a visit to Birmingham Town Hall to see Field Marshal J.C. Smuts receive the Freedom of the City. Subsequently, a distinguished Old Edwardian, Field Marshal Sir William J. Slim of Burma fame also received the Freedom of the City and school was proud to be given the day off in his honour. Our freedom to roam around the city that afternoon had been safeguarded by the men in his largely forgotten 14th Army. I remember the son of our next door neighbour returning from service against the Japanese and he died within weeks.

The war had greatly affected my schooling but had far greater consequences for many born a year or so earlier.

19. MY SCHOOL EXPERIENCES – A MIDDLE CLASS EDUCATION

Gerald Marsh

I was born on the 5th November 1925 and christened at Kings Norton Parish Church, Birmingham. My story begins differently from most of my contemporaries because almost seven years were to elapse before attendance at school began. At 4$\frac{1}{2}$ years of age I developed mastoiditis, which was at first misdiagnosed. Two operations on my left ear took place in the family home at Wavertree, Liverpool, followed by a death defying third in a nursing home at West Kirby, near Hoylake, Cheshire, where my father had taken the family of 8 for a holiday.

The nursing procedures of the time, where children were thought to be knowledgeable young adults, left me with phobia symptoms which stayed with me for many years afterwards. There were no antibiotics, wounds were cauterised no matter how sensitive the area. This was not a normal progression to a grown-up environment. The adverse effects, together with "The Delicate Child Syndrome" were to be revealed as contrary to my natural disposition as an adventurous boy. In late 1931, I attended Caulderstones Preparatory School (Miss Bell's), Liverpool, where I was treated with concern and kindness.

In 1932, father was promoted and in consequence we moved back to Birmingham from where I had been carried (December 1925) as a babe-in-arms. We moved into 21 St. Agnes Road, Moseley, and my next schooling was at the early buildings (now demolished) of Bedford College, 57 Wake Green Road, run by Mrs. Coombs, B.A. and Miss Bedford. Here I learnt to write on a Welsh slate, probably to save paper. My report at the end of the Winter term shows that I was exposed to 16 subject topics.

After the Summer term of 1933, my brother John (2 years older) moved with me to Woodroughs School for Boys, which was housed at Greenhill House standing in its own grounds at the top of Ascot Road, Moseley, a cul-de-sac. A Mr. W. Hawkes, M.A., was Headmaster. The school uniform, obtained from Dunn's the outfitters in the city, comprised a green jacket with yellow and green piped trims with the school badge on the pocket – a Lion Rampant. The green peaked cap had the same piping and a smaller badge. Grey worsted trousers were mandatory and each winter the younger boys pressurised their parents to put them into long trousers because sometimes the classrooms were so cold. This was not the only reason, for long trousers were a grown up status symbol.

However, the reason given was often true as radiators or boilers were often on the blink, and it was always cold on Monday mornings, as one might expect. There were coal fires in most rooms but they were inadequate (especially for those sitting by the draughty windows), and they had to be made up by ourselves as the janitor was often too busy. When cold, I could not concentrate; in this I was not alone.

The school fees were five guineas a term. It was here that I first played football and cricket – Moseley College was our main rival. The football ground was in Windermere Road, at the Yardley Wood Road end. A biplane landed on this field in 1934 and we were required to remove the goal posts so that the pilot could take off again. For cricket we had a smoother field of mown grass on the opposite side of Yardley Wood Road, behind the Corporation Depot which housed the massive road repair steam rollers. About 30 of these monsters would steam out in the mornings to various parts of the city and return before darkness descended to where we were waiting for them. From a bench and table outside our tuck shop we held shaken up ginger beer (clay) bottles and would untwist the wire holding the corks in place at the crucial moment to hit the boilers about 15 feet away!

Our literature and scripture teacher was silver-haired Miss Wilson who related to us individually. Her only rivals were the mice which came out of the skirting boards, their antics distracted our attention. We begged her not to report their presence as they were not on the register – so we all lived happily together. I found I was quite good at sports, winning the 100 yds sprint three years in succession. Teaching wise, when not doing so well in a subject, I developed an unfortunate philosophy to counteract the unimaginative comments on end of term reports, such as "Could do better": "Requires more application"; "Will do well if he tries harder". This philosophy was not to worry, as we would probably be moving away soon.

The real truth was that I was studying the teachers, rather than the matters which they were endeavouring to teach me. Deep in my subconscious I had begun to develop lateral thinking, many years before Edward de Bono wrote his book. Just how stupid can a young boy be? However, we were taught not to criticise our elders, who had a mystical claim to being superior, and believe it or not asking questions was sometimes thought to be impertinent unless asked in a diffident manner, which was not me. Keeping thoughts to myself I suffered the disadvantage of giving a poorer performance than that of which I was capable.

Sure enough in 1936 my father was made a Company Director and we moved to Leicester. Loss of school friends did not worry me unduly for my philosophy warned me to expect such events. However, children love new experiences.

We moved to a lovely house at 354 London Road, three miles from the Market Cross. We built up a menagerie of many pets. Two miles away was the best designed open air swimming pool that I have ever seen, even to this day. It had high diving boards to Olympic specification, set in a concrete structure above 18 feet of water. The semi-circular pool was surrounded by grassed rose arbours, like separate rooms, open at one side, with views across the pool into open countryside beyond. We all spent many hours there.

Three brothers, with myself, attended Wyggeston Grammar School. The fees were 8 guineas a term. Uniform was a plain black jacket with school badge and grey trousers. The peaked black cap had a smaller badge and had a silver/white cord over the crown. There were 800 boys attending at this time.

Administratively the school was divided into Senior and Junior branches: Mr. T. E. Kingdom, M.A., was headmaster. My two older brothers, Gordon and John, were placed in the Senior whilst myself and a younger brother, Arthur, were in the Junior School. Pupils had to earn promotion into the Senior School. There were designated sports houses, Latimer, Wycliffe, Went and Whites. All pupils were allocated to a house which lasted all one's school days. All success points from both Seniors and Junior were totalled so that the whole school strove to be the top house of the year. There were more teachers here than I could keep track of, which was a good aspect.

An incident showed me that I still had built-in trauma. My first form master was Mr. E. Chadd, whom I liked. During a spelling session he asked me to spell accommodation and recommendation – I put one C in accommodation and was brought to the front of the class of 28. He held my right arm at the biceps and asked me again. I was confused and hesitated. He dug his fingers deeply into my muscle. I lifted my left arm high and brought it down with some force on to his left arm, breaking free. Returning to my seat I fixed him with a most ferocious look. He recovered some composure and went on with the lesson, which soon came to an end as it was mid-morning break. For a week I was hero of the Junior School. All were predicting a caning from the Head but I think Chadd realised that he had gone a bit too far and the incident was forgotten.

It did, however, have an unexpected outcome. There was a bully, whom

I did not rate, operating in the Junior School. In his mind I had, by this incident, become top-gun. He and his mates 'roughed up' my younger brother and took his school cap. I was given the message that it could be retrieved, after school, behind the bicycle sheds. When I arrived he had assembled his six member gang and stood there grinning. I strode up to him and fetched him such a blow to the jaw that his teeth started to bleed. He cowed down, I took back Arthur's cap and the others melted away. A few days later several boys asked me to form a gang. I told them not to be so daft and that everyone should stand on their own feet. If they wanted to play tough they should do so on the rugby field. We heard no more of gangs.

The senior maths teacher was known as chicken, because when he walked his head nodded up and down in a sort of pecking motion – he had bright red hair. One day I saw him dive off the top board at Kenwood pool – some chicken!

My form master (Senior School) was for some time in the trenches of World War I, which left him with permanent shell-shock, with good and bad days. Although harmless he sometimes suffered baffled rages, almost like commencing an apoplectic fit, stopping in his tracks with a grimace on his face. Not a pretty sight, poor chap – but he was a good teacher. When a boy threw a paper dart or shot a paper pellet he would sometimes put the wrong boy in detention. Detention meant staying after school for half an hour, during which time you produced a letter, addressed to the Headmaster, saying why you were there and how contrite you were. Very difficult if you had done nothing!

The Reverend Lewis took us for scripture and latin. He was a clergyman on Sundays but a terrorist to schoolboys for the rest of the week, in or out of classes. One day in class he took a swipe at a boy's head. The boy collapsed and it was mandatory that the matron was fetched. Next day the parents came to see the Headmaster. The Reverend's loss of face and quieter manner was a joy to behold.

We had good workshops for woodwork and metalwork. Selecting our own projects from design sheets we were required to work strictly to them.

During these years at Wyggeston I was picked, usually with another boy, not always the same one but always me, by the Leicester Education Authority for a monitoring activity. I had to attend their offices and answer printed multi-choice questions. This was between 1937 and 1939. (I believe such papers are in general use now – but were certainly not for written examinations at school at this time). All this gave me some stress as I was never able to find out how I fared and what the purpose of the exercise was. There were pupils from other Leicester schools, who were told no more than I was.

In our family life an ordered regime was drawing to a close. My paternal grandmother was put into a nearby nursing home where she died, aged 89. My mother had looked after her for 21 years whilst tending her own children.

World War II

On the 3rd September 1939, sitting in St. John the Baptist Anglican Church, Clarendon Park Road, we were sadly ill at ease. The Vicar placed his wireless set on the pulpit to hear Neville Chamberlain make the announcement that we were now at war with Germany. My elder brother who had left Wyggeston in 1937 had joined the R.A.F.V.R., training after work at Ansty Aerodrome. On September 1st he was called up for active service. Father was very grave; he had served in the first World War. Mother had lost two brothers at the front, one blown up by a shell fired after 11 a.m. on the 11th November 1918 as he struck the gong for the men to come for mid-day dinner.

Things moved rapidly after the war announcement. On the playing fields at Wyggeston we had to dig trenches for air raid shelters, which were hundreds of yards long. Workmen directed by the Ministry of Defence came and erected reinforced concrete beams to form interlocking archways. As each section was finished we shovelled and packed the heavy clay soil down each side and over the top. Inside wooden forms were along each side facing each other about 4' apart. Low wattage lamps powered by car batteries lit each section.

In late 1939, father's organisation had many staffing problems; men at every level, including very senior men who were reserve officers, were now being called up. It became necessary for him to move back to Birmingham. The household followed him in October 1940. Once again my dread prophesy had become fact and so ended four years of continuous education, the longest period which I ever experienced.

At Birmingham I found myself turned down by King Edward's School at Bristol Road, Edgbaston, because I was of an unsuitable age to fit in and had missed the date for September's intake. My elder brother, John, and younger brother, Arthur, were accepted and did well. Eventually I was placed at King Edward's Grammar School, Five Ways. My thoughts were set on joining the O.T.C. as a first step towards joining the armed forces. On my first day I found that the O.T.C. had been evacuated to Monmouth School in Wales with the main body of pupils.

Frustrated, I spent some unproductive months with teachers to whom I did not relate at all well. Some had been brought out of retirement and one was a conscientious objector who was supposed to act as our sports master.

At the sports ground in Portland Road we found that he did not know the rules of rugby football, but he had a whistle. The Latin teacher, who could quote verbatim our set book "Latin for To-day" did not teach in a manner helpful to understanding the structure of the language. Not much was learnt, except perhaps mathematics and practice at drawing.

Whilst talking with classmates in the playground, a boy whom I did not know, came up behind me and hit me hard over the crown of my head with a cut-off piece of heavy weight hose which he had found. I saw stars, was almost unconscious, buckling at the knees. I put my hands on the ground and steadied myself. Looking round and up I saw just another grinning boy (like Cook at Wyggeston). Starting from low down I straightened my legs and planted such a punch on his jaw which lifted him off his feet and stretched him on his back unconscious. The matron was summoned and I was branded as the guilty party and told to report forthwith to the Assistant Head, known as Peg-leg Fulford (the Head, C. H. Dobinson, was at Monmouth). I convinced him that I was not the guilty party and he seemed more concerned to see the other boy was taken off to the Children's Hospital next door in Ladywood Road.

During 1941 my brother Gordon had been reported missing in action. He had two more flights to do before becoming an instructor to train new pilots. One night just before we had the telegram informing us of this, my mother had woken up inconsolable – she had heard Gordon calling her. It was later confirmed in a letter from his C.O. who said that radio contact was lost when his plane was returning over the North Sea – at 11 p.m., the same time my mother had woken. Some weeks later the Red Cross from Geneva had received information from the Dutch that his body had been found on the beach at Ness, near a small village on the Island of Arneland off the coast of Holland. After this shock I lost interest in everything. It was the only time when I ever heard my father cry – he had lost his eldest son, who was the standard bearer of his hopes for all his family, at just 21 years of age.

I was coming up to 16 years of age and was told by my parents not to set my heart on joining the services as I was unlikely to pass the medical because of my history. I went to see the Air Raid Warden and enlisted in the Fire Watch rota – later I was to help put out three incendiary bombs.

My brother John received the pass results from K.E.S. for the General School Certificate and wanted to sit for Higher School Certificate before he was called up. The only way he could achieve this was to take the next sitting in one year's time so father sent him to Lawrence's College in Corporation Street. Here he seemed to progress well and it was thought that the same place would help me as K.E. Five Ways did not. It was, to me, a cramming establishment, bent on nothing but the highest pass rates to enhance their reputation and improve a private business. They did not find a suitable, willing and competent slave in me. The two teachers were indifferent and rude and I was most unhappy. However, I am pleased to report that John passed his H.S. Certificate at the first sitting and went on to an engineering course at Birmingham University.

All these experiences did nothing for my confidence, so father, ever concerned to do the best for all his remaining children, found a small private tutorial group centred in a flat at Five Ways. Here I studied for examinations set by the College of Preceptors and achieved three certificates up to the level of Oxford & Cambridge School Certificate. This pleased father, but knowing myself that the fees were high, I asked to leave. (Father was being taxed at 19/6d in the £1 for much of his income). It was 1942 and the end of my informal schooldays.

In 1943 I began work at Morris Commercial Cars at Adderley park; I worked long hours helping to build vehicles for the forces, ambulances and beach assault craft known as "Ducks" which were powered by four Ford V8 engines. They were tested at Castle Bromwich – some of them were used in "D-Day" landings. One evening per week and weekends once a fortnight I trained as a private in the Home Guard 27th battery "A" Company No. 3 Platoon, Royal Warwickshire Regiment.

It may seem strange to some people that our family took no part in Victory celebrations (of course, as politicians hasten to say, we were glad and relieved that it was over) but there was sadness in our hearts for what might have been our futures if there had been no war.

Truly things would never be the same as in 1938.

20. NEVER AN OPERA DIVA

Gladys Levy

O n delving into the recesses of my mind, it was obvious from the start that I was not going to be an opera singer. My first teacher told me not to sing on the grounds that I grunted. At my next school where the choir was performing "The Lady of Shalott" in cantata form, I was tested for the choir and was told to sing up the scale. Petrified, not a sound came out. Was I humiliated?

At an early school medical examination I was exhorted to stand up straight or I would never take after my mother. They were quite right – my mother was described as "a fine figure of a woman" and a very dignified lady.

We had swimming lessons at public baths and I still have visions of the great black beetles in the water. Being a timid child I demurred on being told to jump in, so I was pushed in. However, I struck out and to my amazement found I could actually swim. What joy!

My geography lessons were haunted by the fear that my teacher would notice that I had stuck two pages of my exercise book together to conceal the enormous blot I had made which spread evilly over the page. I still see that monstrous blot, but the teacher refrained from comment.

One punishment at this school was to stand under the clock at break in full view of everyone passing. For one of my misdemeanours I stood there one day when, to my chagrin, I saw my brother approaching and I knew he would rush home and tell tales to our mother. Great was my delight to find he too had instructions to "Stand under the clock", so neither of us sneaked on the other on that occasion, but I never found out what his sin had been.

The Salvation Army was much in evidence in London in those days and frequently on my way home from school I was greeted by one of their enthusiasts. He was a dwarf-like man, named Sid, who always wore a large brown cap. He tried hard to persuade me to "Come and Join us", not because of the good work which the Army undoubtedly did, but because he thought I would look "so attractive in the bonnet". I resisted his blandishments.

I was an avid reader in those days and one day was caught in class reading "All Quiet on the Western Front" under the desk when I should have been concentrating on something entirely different. The book had only recently been published, so my teacher confiscated it on the grounds that it was not suitable reading for a child of my years! I am convinced that she circulated it to all members of the staff before returning the book to me.

My fondest recollection of my schooldays is of being taken out one morning as a reward and being presented with a propelling pencil and a crossword puzzle book – an event which started me off on a lifetime of addiction.

21. A SCIENTIFIC HEAD BOY

Stan Jones

It was late in August 1939. War clouds which had been gathering on the horizon, broke. Waverley Grammar School was recalled from the summer holiday and on September 1st 1939 we took the train from Small Heath to Evesham. Memory of that first day remains vivid. It was extremely hot when we finally arrived at the Grammar School in Evesham. We were given hot cocoa! We were trailed round Evesham and up Greenhill and because there were no billets, a group of us had to sleep on a mattress on the floor of the Abbey Manor. Breakfast consisted of bully beef and tea made with condensed milk.

After about a week, my cousin (who had just started at Waverley) and I were billeted on one of the largest market gardeners in Evesham. It was an "Upstairs, downstairs" situation. At first we lived with the servants, but after Christmas 1939, my cousin returned to Birmingham and I spent more time with the family. This was a pleasant time and vastly widened my experience. The climax was that my hostess paid for me to take her thirteen year old daughter to the pictures on a number of occasions!

Living now in an area famous for its market gardens, I was able to take advantage of some of the seasonal farming jobs available. For instance, I went pea picking which boosted my pocket money nicely. I was paid one shilling and six pence per sack. There were gypsies employed also, but they remained aloof, concentrating on the picking – a serious business for them on which their living depended.

Waverley pupils used the Evesham school premises during the afternoons only, so we rarely met the local children and there was no rivalry to speak of. Retired teachers returned, replacing those on war service. For my part, the School Certificate Examinations were looming ever closer and after that I expected to return home, as the long awaited air raids had not yet materialised. Amidst all the upheaval, in July 1940 I took and obtained School Certificate and went home to Birmingham.

In September 1940 I started in the sixth form at Birmingham studying science for Higher School Certificate. But now the phony war had ended and our studies were interrupted by constant air raids. At the end of November it was decided to evacuate part of the school to Melton Mowbray in Leicestershire. Because it was only there that sixth form study was available, in December I decided to go. There I spent the best part of two very happy years.

I lived at first in the beautiful home of the Secretary of the local Building Society (and a Methodist preacher) and then at a farm house which was the home of the Officer of the Ministry of Agriculture. During the second year there, school was held in a lovely country house next to the local Grammar school. There were only four of us in the sixth form, so we established our own Annexe, where we retained our Waverley study habits and uniform.

To our dismay the Chemistry master had been called up so the Mathematics master agreed to supervise our work. In addition, the Physics master had remained in Birmingham, though he saw to it that a good standard textbook was made available. The shortage of teachers entailed a great deal of private study. We had the use of the neighbouring school for laboratory work and for games. During 1941-42 there had been two hard snowy winters and two lovely summers and Double Summertime.

Short of apparatus at one time, we returned on the bus to Birmingham to borrow some from school. Since one section of the apparatus consisted of a large glass tube about three feet long, together with other bulky parts, the struggle to transport it caused quite a sensation on the return journey. Surprisingly, it reached Melton intact and was most useful once installed.

Life was not all work; we took part in some of the local activities, becoming regular members of the Air Training Corps, and were also invited to join the school's table tennis club, which I enjoyed.

Once again, important exams were approaching, and a final flurry of studies occupied our attention. In July 1942 I finished up as Head Boy and with a Higher School Certificate, which enabled me to go to University.

22. AT SCHOOL IN THE GARDEN OF ENGLAND

Sheila Barnes

The brick built National School in St. Mary Cray, Orpington, Kent, was built in 1909 although a school had existed before this date on the same site from Victorian times. Outside toilets, the norm, were at the end of an enclosed school playground. 'Girls & Infants' on one side and 'Boys' on the other. A central hall, from which led off six class rooms, catered for the village children. Pegs and wash-basins led off this hall and a small room was also available to teach the local Romany, peripatetic scholars, when they could be spared from pea-picking, hopping, strawberry picking, potato lifting and apple picking. They had their breakfasts, cornflakes and milk, and were encouraged to have a good wash at the hand basins. The 3 Rs were then attended to.

Early sewing and knitting were taught to the girls and heating was in the form of a fire in the corner of the room. On winter days the milk was put round the fire guard to take off the chill. Above the fireplace was a Dutch interior of "Women peeling apples" by Vermeer. In the sewing room it was a Raeburn of 'Boy with a Rabbit'. An early appreciation of art was generated in schools at that time.

The Headmaster, music master (who also looked after the Romany children), and two male teachers were a high proportion of the male/female staff. The Headmaster came to school wearing a lounge suit and bowler hat – how different from today's T-shirt and jeans image! We celebrated Empire Day and in the school hall was a bronze plaque of scholars who had given their lives in the 1914-18 war. Poppy day was always observed. Plays and a school percussion orchestra performed at Christmas and a dancing teacher came in from Orpington on Friday evenings to teach the girls to tap dance for a small fee.

In 1940, the top class had a high proportion of children successful in the 11+ or scholarship exams. 3 boys and 2 girls went to Chislehurst and Sidcup Grammar School and 1 boy and 4 girls went to Bromley Grammar School. At that time there were no grammar schools in Orpington and St. Olave's had not moved down from London to the present country site. We

had an outing to the London Zoo and Madame Tussaud's in our last year, and one boy got left on the tube train, causing great panic, from Regent's Park. He got off at the next station from where a teacher retrieved him.

War time exploits didn't really impinge at that early state and deep shelters were dug in the adjoining Recreation Ground, and it was later on at Grammar School where the Blitz, the V1 and V2 rockets wrought havoc on our Secondary School education, but we managed to obtain our School Certificates with no "counselling".

I had to take two buses, one from St. Mary Cray to Sidcup and a further bus from Sidcup to Chislehurst to get to school. Another girl from the village and I used to travel together. Even in war time our parents did not take us. The school sustained bomb damage and at one time the school ran Monday, Wednesday and Friday one week with prep at home on the Tuesday and Thursday, and vice-versa on the following week.

There were two parallel forms all the way up the school until the VIth form when there were just Lower and Upper VIth, many girls leaving at 16 to earn their livings.

We had deep shelters dug at the beginning of the playing fields and my first French lesson contained the vocabulary 'la masque à gaz' and 'le banc' as we sat on benches on either side of the trenches, which had no heating and were very ill lit. P.E. was hilarious, with a very tall Gym teacher doing drill exercises and touching the ceilings easily. We took iron rations down there, as well as our gas masks. Chocolate, Ovaltine tablets and small packets of biscuits were part of the staple diet.

Once when the siren sounded at Sidcup Police Station, my friend and I were waiting at the bus stop and our German teacher, Miss Milton, who lodged opposite the bus stop, came and made us shelter in her front room under the table. Radar had just started and strips of silver paper were dropped to minimise the effectiveness and we saw this on the way to school, but our mothers had always told us never to touch anything, but this didn't apply to shrapnel, of which I had quite a collection.

Being very near Biggin Hill we saw many dog fights overhead and I well remember my School Certificate exams in the Gym, with windows heavily netted and sticky tape in a cross pattern to stop glass splinters flying. It was at the height of the Buzz-Bomb period and when the invigilator heard one she would click a stopwatch, say "Under your desks, girls", and when it had exploded (fortunately past our building), we'd get up and resume our exam, she'd click the stopwatch again and add on all the interruptions to our final time. How we passed I do not know, but children are very resilient.

Domestic Science lessons were very basic, with rationing, but our Scottish Cookery teacher was very resourceful. I learned of V.E. day in

May during her lesson. We had a mock election, so were introduced to politics. We went up to see 'Macbeth' given by Donald Wolfit's Company in London, which was our set Shakespeare play, and also had a travelling theatre group come to give us George Bernard Shaw's 'Candida' in the school hall. I also remember a fascinating talk on Chaucer from a dashing Captain from ABCA, the Army Bureau of Current Affairs. Also, as in our primary school, paintings by the Great Masters abounded in our formrooms and in the corridors, so our art appreciation was not forgotten. Music was played prior to school assemblies and the standard of our singing was very high, with a Senior and Junior Choir. A school drama society, stamp club, gardening club (Dig for Victory) were also extra-curricular activities. We managed to play matches with other local schools and our teachers were marvellous in giving us a normal background in an abnormal time. We all had to stick to school uniform even though coupons were required.

We had gymslips, blue blouses and a pullover in winter, and check dresses in green, blue or yellow with white collars and cuffs in the summer. Panama hats, velour hats and berets for cyclists were worn and Melton cloth coats or raincoats with a blazer in the summer. The school outfitter, Graham Gardiner from Leicester, came at the beginning of the autumn term to measure us all in the Sick Room. We collected bus tickets and ones with a number seven on them were considered lucky for some obscure reason.

Nicknames for school dinners were often quite descriptive – blood and bones for jam tart with strips of pastry, and boiled babies' heads for suet puddings!

Recycling was a necessity during the war, and the girls collected silver paper, newspaper and rose hips for rose hip syrup. With sweet rationing we never had many sweets but it was a heinous offence to eat sweets in school uniform. Often we joined on the end of a queue at the Maypole Dairy in Sidcup to buy a 2d. jelly which we ate in squares to augment our sweet ration.

Local farmers and landowners let us pick up fallen Worcester Permain apples from their orchards, much appreciated by our parents. From VE Day in May the street lights were on again and blanket curtains were not necessary. That was when it finally dawned on me that peace was a fact and I was always slightly shocked to see electric light streaming through the windows in our road. Gas masks still sat on the hooks of the hall stand from force of habit and we never wasted a line of our Rough Note Books or else we weren't issued with another. To this day I still save pieces of string and bits of paper for shopping lists. Habit dies hard!

I remember D-day vividly, when the local arterial road, the A21, was nose to tail with army lorries, heavily camouflaged, all making for the coast and we realised something 'Very Big' was on. The serious mien of the drivers' faces and the continuous rumble of the engines and sheer inevitability of the massive convoy brought home the fact that the tide was turning and the Second Front battle was imminent.

For an all round good grounding in English literature, Grammar, Maths, French, German, Geography, History, Art, Music and R.I. there was nothing better than the old grammar schools, and with local technical schools and the central schools each was 'educated according to (their) ability'. With the coming of comprehensive education I believe they are still streamed into nine classes, the top three being taught languages etc. and the bottom three having easier lessons.

A country is pleased to train its élite for top jobs like doctors, lawyers, teachers and lecturers, and engineers, but perhaps there is a non-élitist attitude today. I see no shame in excellence. State Scholarships were a feature of our Honours' Boards and one thought it a great goal to aim for. Our school motto was 'IT IS REQUIRED OF A STEWARD THAT HE BE FOUND FAITHFUL', and this was printed over the stage so at assemblies we saw it every day, and it was a good precept to live by.

23. A Yorkshire Elementary Education

Peggy Timmis

Harehills Elementary School, Leeds – built in 1910, is situated on a main road out of the city, but well out of town, not far from the city boundary. At one end of its catchment area were rows of back to back terraced houses, nearest the city, soon becoming roads of larger Edwardian terraces with front gardens and back yards, on the outer edge was the newly built suburb Gledhow Woods, modern semis with large gardens and tree lined roads. About 2/3 of the pupils came from the streets off the main road and 1/3 from Gledhow.

The school was a large solid building housing infants and juniors up to the age of 9 on the ground floor and boys and girls 9-14 on the upper floor. Each department had a large central assembly hall with the classrooms arranged round the perimeter of the hall.

In 1932 (when I was 10) we had a new Headmaster in the senior school. John William Driver, an extremely tall, very thin man with a military bearing (he had been an officer in the first world war) always wore a black bowler hat and carried a tightly rolled black umbrella when walking to school, summer and winter. Soon after his arrival, morning assembly was changed, instead of one hymn then reciting the Lord's Prayer followed by any notices from the Headmaster plus being urged to work hard at our lessons and behave ourselves, we were back in the classrooms by 9.10 a.m. Now we had a hymn, Lord's Prayer and another hymn, followed by a short talk from the Head, usually history or geography of the British Empire. Then the Union Jack was unfurled, held by 2 boys (never girls) from the top class,chosen by their teacher on the basis of good behaviour and marks obtained during the week. We then all sang the National Anthem returning to our classrooms about 9.30 a.m. There were quite a few Jewish children in the school, and they were excused attendance at hymns and prayers but had to join us for the Head's talk and National Anthem (in the meantime they sat quietly in the classroom – door open – reading the Old Testament).

Mr. Driver, I now realise, was a very kind man, he rarely used to cane the boys (the previous Head used to cane two or three boys every day), but he was fanatically patriotic, Empire Day, May 24th was his big day.

There would be the usual morning assembly but large maps of the world were hung on the walls, and the whole school had to chorus the name of every area of pink on the map as Mr. Driver pointed to it, until we had been over the whole British Empire. The best "reciter" in each class had to stand up and read the most patriotic poems of R. Kipling and others, then we went back to our classrooms for one lesson, usually arithmetic, while the school playground was prepared (if wet in the hall – but I cannot remember a wet day). The boy's playground was used, as the entrance to the boilerhouse was in the girls' playground and there were always great piles of coke around the one side. A small platform (made by the boys in woodwork) was set up, then the piano in the infants' assembly hall was borrowed for the occasion, and was carried out by several of the male teachers and senior boys.

Then the whole senior school assembled in the playground and to the rather faint sounds of the piano we sang "Land of Hope and Glory", "Rule Britannia" and "My Country Tis of Thee" before being drawn up like a military parade, each class led by their own teacher marching in front, and we marched round the playground to military marches on the piano. Each class eventually passed the platform where Mr. Driver stood at attention with the Union Jack. Everyone saluted the flag before being drawn up in a square again to sing the National Anthem. By which time it was 12 o'clock and "Home Time".

There were iron railings at the top end of the playground facing the main road, and many of the parents came to watch. Remember this was the 1930's and the depression had hit the North badly, so there were many fathers at home, most of whom were World War I ex-servicemen, who would remove their hats and stand to attention during the National Anthem.

I feel all this made a deep impression on us children, and I think, now, that it must have shaped our attitudes to service for our country when World War II came only a few years after we had left school.

24. It Never Rained when I went to School

Bill Davies

I was born in the East End in 1925. The district in which I lived was truly a "working class" area. We were not subject to the grinding poverty of, say, Stepney or Poplar, but were hardly "well off" like Wanstead – even according to the standards of the day. Stratford, where I lived, had two major employers – The London & North Eastern Railway (LNER) and the Co-operative Society (Co-op). The LNER had big freight and repair facilities in the town whilst the Co-op maintained major laundry, funeral, milk and coal distribution services. The two organisations came together several times each day when flocks of sheep, herds of cattle and pigs were driven by teams of men and boys from the freight yards along our road to the Co-op slaughter house. Hence we were familiar with the sight of the country although in an urban setting.

To the children of the district the sight of hundreds of animals on the move was perfectly natural. Just as natural were other aspects of life. Engine drivers working out of London enjoyed a very superior rate of pay and were "better off". My mother maintained that you could always tell the difference between the wife of an engine driver and those of the firemen and cleaners. The former were fat like their husbands, the latter were "narrow gutted".

Tragedy both local and national was accepted as usual. "Mr. So & So" was killed last night in the shunting yards: he was squashed between the buffers of a wagon. Mine disasters with loss of life were commonplace; loss of life at sea through vessels sinking even in good weather happened weekly. Occasionally you might witness an ambulance taking a mother to the hospital or sanatorium and you would suspect that it would be unlikely for her to return to her children.

Children accepted that there could be inequalities in life just as there were tragedies. More unusual was the case of Mrs. Brown who lived opposite. Her husband was a burglar. One night he fell from a window and broke his neck. Now she was a widow and her son an orphan.

To add to his troubles he had to wear his cap at all times at school because he suffered from complete alopecia.

One afternoon in September, the airship R101 sailed straight across the top of our house. It was a magnificent sight. The papers the next day carried pictures of what remained after it crashed in France with 48 people dead.

Schooling started at five years of age. Downsell Road School was a typical LCC establishment; a foursquare block with three entrances, infants, juniors and seniors. Three infants classes were admitted each year. Three years at infant level, three each at junior and senior, thus nine years at school leaving at fourteen. Life seemed absolutely predictable and foretold.

Like everyone we took in lodgers to augment income. Living in a corner house we had an entrance to the backyard which my mother let out to costmongers to store their barrows. Among them was "Carbolic Bill". He spent frequent periods as a guest of H.M. the King in Pentonville. When not there he made a sort of living by selling carbolic soap and disinfectant around the district from a pram. His usual dress was a raincoat buttoned to the neck, a dirty brown trilby, and glasses so grubby you could not see his eyes. Added to the pervasive smell of carbolic it was a wonder he did not scare away all business. At the other end of the scale, two men kept motor bikes in the shed. They had Panther machines with highly polished petrol tanks decorated with the emblem of a panther in full chase.

My constant companion was a boy about 18 months older than me who usually had a candle hanging from his nose. It took me five years to realise how gormless he was. He and I were playing on scrubland on Wanstead Flats one afternoon when we were set upon by a party of about six boys. My friend now proved how wrong my opinion of him was because he was off like a shot, leaving me to face the music! I was told that as a captive I would have to fight them all – one at a time – and then they would hang me. Obviously stupid since the string they produced would not have secured a parcel and the branches would not have supported my weight! However, after two fights another gang of slightly older boys burst on the scene and I was off like the panther on the bike!

To my juvenile eyes the world was peopled by characters. However, there was one constant ghostly figure in the background – my father. On one occasion I bought some peanut brittle and a large piece got stuck in my throat. I reeled around our shop gasping for breath just as he came in from work. He immediately put his finger in my mouth, down my throat and extracted the sweet. I can still taste the dust on his finger with thanks. One other comment about him. Although we sold general dry goods, biscuits, bread, sugar, Camp coffee etc. – our main trade was supposed to be that of a corn chandler, which involved keeping supplies of hay and straw in the shop. Once a lad threw a lighted firework in the door. My father caught him and gave him a belt round the ear. Moments later the lad returned with his father demanding to know why his son had been clouted. When told that the firework could have caused a fire in the shop the father then gave the boy another good hiding – two for the price of one.

My mother was soft. She ran the shop whilst my father was at work. It was common practice to allow "tick" and she allowed so much she was having difficulty in paying suppliers. One family managed to run up a bill of £30! But the problem was – cut off credit and never get your money back. That family with the £30 bill – there were 7 children in the family, the eldest aged 7. The father was a navvy. The children were dressed in rags, no socks, worn out scruffy boots and always dirty. The children, predominantly girls, usually looked absolutely petrified. What could be seen of the place where they lived was no better. Even my childish heart sank.

In 1934 we moved to Croydon and school was very different. St. Andrews was a High Anglican Church and great emphasis was put on Religious Instruction at the school. I was a pupil there for two years. Classes were mixed ability and mixed boys and girls. There was no attempt at segregation or streaming until the senior years. If I could make a value judgement between St. Andrews and Downsell Road I would say that in a comparable subject such as arithmetic, St. Andrews was 18 months behind. However, St. Andrews did have a very active Cub and Scout organisation and this, together with other outside interests, made up in my mind for academic deficiencies.

As an aid to discipline the cane was scarcely used at my previous school. However, at St. Andrews it was more in evidence. My teacher, Miss Choppin, like others, was well practised in its use. I have given the idea that academically the school was the pits. Probably it was, but in other ways I gained immeasurably from my time there. I started to soak up elements of the faith of the Church of England; Saint Andrew more than Saint George is the one I cleave to. When my mother died we insisted that she be buried in the pocket handkerchief size space available at the church. Through the Scouts I made friends who remained true until they died. I never lost the ability to walk with kings nor lost the common touch engendered at that place. St. Andrews School may have been most famous for the number of heavyweight boxers and female costermongers it produced, but it also engendered espirit de corps.

At age 10/11 Croydon Education Authority segregated children and also offered scholarships to grammar and central schools. Each year there were 250 places open at the central schools (leaving age 16) and about 25 at the grammar schools (leaving age 18). I was therefore pleased in 1936 to escape the unutterable boredom of Miss Choppin with her pathetic poems about fairies and flowers and join Archbishop Tenison's Central School.

That ghostly figure in the background, my father, was becoming more distinct and helping me to accomplish more adult tasks, urging me on to succeed. Two incidents stand out. Without informing my mother, I went after school, to a friend's birthday party and arrived home four hours late. Mother was in a panic, father had been to the police station! When asked where I had been I correctly said "To Norman's birthday party", adding that I had told my sister. From upstairs she shouted "He did not". Two seconds later I felt it. It was as if my head had been detached from my shoulders by a plank of wood and the word "LIAR" substituted!

There were a fair number of kids living in our road and as always competition to be "top dog". Eventually I finished up fighting outside our back gate. A solid ring of children formed so that it was impossible to break off without losing face. The fight got more furious and then I caught sight of my father standing in the gateway, hands in pockets, grinning all over his face. I could imaging that he was saying "Keep going. If you get hurt it will do you no harm, if you win I will not embarrass you". Happily the sister of the other lad came down the road and shouted "Norman, mum wants you. NOW". We broke off; honour was saved for both of us.

My new school was completely different from St. Andrews. Firstly it was all boys. Secondly the head was J. R. Henderson. What! You have never heard of J. R. Henderson? His only aim in life was to produce more and better school examination results year by year. By and large he succeeded.

One drawback for me was the fact that due to the entry being by scholarship, the boys came from all over Croydon and so out of school friendship was impossible. For the first time I had woodwork instruction; went swimming weekly at the local baths, and regularly played cricket and football on a nearby pitch. As well as keeping contact with Scouts at St. Andrews I was now able to go for trips on the second hand bicycle I had purchased with my earnings from paper rounds, etc.

Life, however, was becoming serious. School uniform had to be looked after. Homework was freely set and had to be completed on time; each year we were entered for several RSA and City & Guilds examinations. The competitive urge to be first (or at worst second) in the class examination lists increased. We were made aware that Archbishop Tenison's was an old foundation in Croydon (12 poor boys, 12 poor girls, 300 years, etc.), and that although not quite as ancient nor as wealthy as Whitgift Grammar, should be regarded with pride and we should do nothing detrimental to the good name of the school.

Then came the War

I still had 18 months to go before leaving examinations could be taken. There was no certainty that they would be held. Education in Croydon was suspended, all staff were being relocated at the place chosen for evacuation, and I went with the school to Crowborough, a town near Tonbridge Wells.

The first three months were a scholastic shambles. We were first crammed with another school of evacuees in to the local village school.

Our next classroom was the bowls hut on the village green. Finally we took over a large house, Craigmore Hall, on the edge of town. At this time, J. R. Henderson, the guiding force in the school, was struck down for several months by some infection. Members of staff were being called to military service and those left also has to cope with billeting problems.

Towards the end of 1940, I found out that my particular hero among the staff, the French teacher, was a homosexual – with leanings towards me. I had no great difficulty in avoiding his attentions but I was left feeling disillusioned and let down.

December 1940 was the end of my school days. I rode to the station on my bicycle, by now battered beyond repair, and I left it propped against the booking office and returned to Croydon. With regret I said goodbye to Crowborough. Without parental restriction I had roamed for miles in the Ashdown Forest; I had witnessed dog fights over the Weald of Kent; I had seen the New Zealanders and others prepare defences against invasion. Unfortunately I had at the most critical time also seen a decline in academic standards since mid-1939, obviously caused by the upheavals of war. Only half of the original class finished their education. With them I returned home clutching my Oxford School Certificate with Matriculation exemption.

I had not let down J. R. Henderson. *Goodbye Schooling.*

Hello Education

Within a few days I was in uniform, clutching a rifle! That ghostly figure who had been absent for the last year and a half, enrolled me in the Home Guard unit operating from Archbishop Tenison's School – full circle. A few days later I was working in London in the Blitz and had enrolled on a three night per week course at Regent Street Polytechnic.

I came to realise what a significant role my father had played in my education for life, particularly as a teacher by example. None of that would have really counted without the schooling of earlier days, however.

Postscript:

St Andrews School was demolished after the war to make room for a ring road. It moved half a mile uphill to the west and now attracts pupils from all over Surrey.

Archbishop Tenison's also moved after the war. Again up hill, this time to the east. It was expanded sixfold into new purpose-built accommodation. However, instead of attracting the best from all over Surrey, it regularly figures as an OFSTED failure, attracting in that role the attention of early morning T.V.

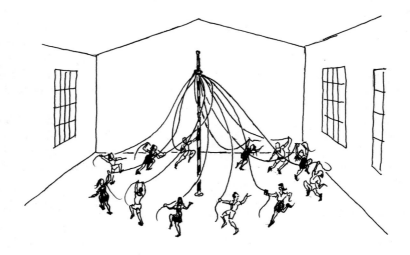

25. Birmingham Schooldays

Ernest Mountford

I celebrated my 5th birthday on the 2nd September 1931 and so I imagine I started school either on or very near that date. I went to Foundry Road School in Winston Green, a typical elementary school of Birmingham, two departments, Juniors and Infants. No playing fields, just a concrete playground. We played no organised games, there was no sporting equipment. We occasionally had P.T. sessions, but these were exercises, again without equipment.

I recall very little of the teaching in the first year at school. I do remember being taught to knit, a small square which we then used as a duster to clean our slates. We wrote with chalk on slates for the first year or two and then we were promoted to paper, pencils and eventually pens. We wrote on lined paper and were taught how to slope our letters and achieve thin and thick lines with the aid of steel nibs.

The Headmaster of the Junior School, Mr. Griffiths, was very keen on arithmetic. The first half hour of every school day in the lower form was taken up in writing our tables. By the time we were 8 or 9 we were all capable of answering any question in our tables up to 12 times. Every Friday afternoon we had an arithmetic test.

The Headmaster had a habit of walking into a classroom and, after asking the teacher's permission, would present the class with some sort of numeracy test. Once he asked us how long the playground was and after several wild guesses he marched us out and measured it. On another occasion he took a chalk and wrote on the blackboard – from 3 take 1 – and we called out 2; take away another 1 – answer 1, take away another 1 – nought; take away another one – silence, then a hesitant "can't do it, sir". He then introduced us to the mystery of minus numbers. I imagine everyone leaving the school would not only be proficient in arithmetic but would also have an interest in numbers.

I have said we had no games or sports equipment, but we did have a maypole. In the middle of the school hall was a deep hole with a metal cover and the maypole fitted into this. Long coloured ribbons dangled from the top and about a dozen boys and girls each held one of the ribbons. We learned various dancing routines, skipping around the pole and weaving in and out of each other; each routine would eventually produce a different pattern from the ribbons. Maypole dancing was part of a May Day celebration.

Another big event was the annual Oxford v Cambridge boat race. A wireless was brought into the school and we all sat crosslegged on the hall floor and listened to the commentary.

In 1937, aged 11, I went to George Dixon Grammar School. Leaving from Foundry Road this was a great culture shock. The School was much bigger, more modern; we had a well equipped gymnasium – and no girls. We had to buy our own textbooks, the masters wore gowns (just like those in the Magnet), the Headmaster was known as The Beak, and we moved around to different rooms for different lessons. It took a while to absorb all the novelty and feel settled but after the first term I began to enjoy it. It was exciting to learn a new language (no one in my family knew a word of French) and to discover that maths was more than just arithmetic. There were science laboratories, a woodworking room and an art classroom with special desks and drawing boards. Outside on the playing fields the main attraction was the horse who pulled the roller. Occasionally the groundsman allowed us to sit on the roller to add to the weight – that was a rare treat.

The two years I was there before the war started, seem in retrospect, to be all summer. We played rugger in winter but I recall much more vividly the cricket matches of summer. The first year, I played in short grey trousers but then my father decided his cricket days were over and he took his flannels to a tailor to be cut down for me. My older sister's boy friend showed me how to oil a bat and to bind the splice with glued string. We played games on Saturday mornings, which meant that with extra homework at weekends, we had little spare time.

The big annual event of the pre-war years was Commemoration day celebration. This was held in the summer term; a huge marquee was erected on the playing field where tea was served to all parents; the athletics finals were run, the school band played, and those not involved in other events gave a marching display. The head of the P.T. staff was, I suspect now, a retired army man and he used to take us outside frequently to rehearse marching manoeuvres.

As regards the races, one, especially, sticks in my mind. It was the mile, four circuits of the track. One runner went off from the start like a rocket and soon had half a lap lead. This was offputting for most of the others but one of them obviously had a plan and stuck to it. He ran steadily checking his time regularly from his wristwatch and gradually hauled his way back in to the race and won. The sprinter could not maintain his speed for a full mile and was eventually overtaken but came second. He then ran behind the pavilion and was violently sick.

With the outbreak of war everything changed. Firstly we were evacuated to Gloucester. Everything at the school was organised and practised as evacuation had been anticipated for some time. We were told what clothes to take and in addition to our gas masks, we were told to buy water bottles in case water supplies were immediately disrupted. One day we were all taken on to the playing fields with our suitcases, gas masks over one shoulder and the water bottle over the other, and we were formed up in orderly lines, split into groups of 8 and pretended to climb in to railway carriages.

When the day came, everything worked perfectly and we arrived safely in Gloucester to find there was plenty of water, which was a pleasant surprise. There was one snag – no-one had arranged accommodation for us. We were split into groups of about 20 with a master and marched around the Gloucester streets, knocking on doors enquiring if anyone would take in evacuees. Fortunately we all found a bed before nightfall.

We were in Gloucester Cathedral on Sunday, the 3rd September, when the service was interrupted to relay the message that war had been declared.

Whilst there, we had the use of a Gloucester school. George Dixon boys and staff had the run of the school for the mornings and the Gloucester boys had lessons in the afternoons.

Most of us left Gloucester at Christmas and our own school re-opened. Some boys and staff were left in Gloucester and so we shared our school premises with Handsworth Grammar School. They were in a similar position with a number of boys and staff away and so again we only worked half a day, with Handsworth using our premises the other half.

Many activities were curtailed during the war years; part of the sports ground was dug up and used to grow vegetables but we still managed some rugger and cricket. Many members of staff went in to the forces and in my last year there I had a lady teacher, which until then was completely unknown. Till then, apart from kitchen staff, the only lady in school was the Head's secretary.

One morning during the raids of 1940/41 we arrived at school to find that a large bomb had fallen in City Road, almost opposite the school. Blast walls around the school had been toppled but the windows and buildings were still intact. In assembly the Headmaster had a terrible announcement to make. The Head Boy of the school, his younger brother who also attended the school, and all the rest of the family had been in one of the houses and all were killed. I think until then, the war had been an exciting lark to most of us but the event brought it home and the whole school was shocked. Incidentally that Head Boy was the lad who came second in the mile race related earlier.

Looking back I realise how dedicated, hard working and enlightened were the teachers of those years. In the elementary school, with very few facilities, teaching children from a very poor part of the city must have been very difficult. At 11, however, we were certainly numerate and also able to write a passable essay. We were taught some poetry – and hymns and psalms.

At Grammar School the staff were not only very capable but imaginative. In music we were taught to sing comic songs – only later we were told they came from Gilbert & Sullivan operas. We listened to records and were encouraged to give our opinions as to the meaning of the sounds – again only later we were told of the Symphony or Concert piece and the composer. In English we studied a small book of short stories. One was by Dorothy L. Sayers and featured Lord Peter Wimsey and this led me to a lifetime of enjoyment in detective fiction.

My school career terminated abruptly. Shortly before the end of my last term I arrived at school to find it under water with broken glass lying around everywhere. On arrival we were all given buckets and mops and shovels and set about clearing up the mess caused by an incendiary bomb attack during the night. After mopping up, the senior boys were sent out on a scouting expedition over the playing fields and across the flat roofs of the school looking for unexploded bombs. We found several and dropped sandbags on them to render them harmless.

After this we were told to clear our desks. We cut off lengths of window cord to tie up our books, said our goodbyes, and that was the end of my academic career.

26. FINAL THOUGHTS

Janet Morris

The exercise of recalling episodes from our childhood and schooldays has forced us all to think, quite carefully, about what our education did for us; whether it enabled us to go on to higher education, enter a profession or one of the many vocational 'callings' (many of which, in those days, could be entered without university degrees) or to work in a worthwhile occupation, frequently followed by marriage and the raising of a family. Our group's experience has encompassed all of these. We have, in our midst, those who have been teachers, doctors, nurses, clerks, caterers, engineers and in many other worthwhile roles. Most of us have brought up families (and see this as the most important job in life) and we thank God to be part of a generation largely untroubled by unemployment.

Other things also emerged which we recognise as having had considerable bearing on our lives. The kind of teaching most of us had, whilst formal and often rigid, taught us the way to acquire knowledge. The INTERNET was still far away but we did know how to use books and libraries and how to record the knowledge gained in clear English. Most of us found that our teachers and peers influenced our thinking as much, if not more than, the subjects we were taught. Above all, the effects of being born in the aftermath of one catastrophic war and living through a second one have obliged us to survive by being adaptable and using whatever resources we could find.

We are thankful for the schools (many of which have gone or are drastically changed) and the many teachers, now mostly dead, who helped and supported us through days which, whilst often happy, were anything but easy. Our concern for the future, as we approach the millennium, is that education will continue to serve the needs of to-day's children, to whom this collection of memories is dedicated.

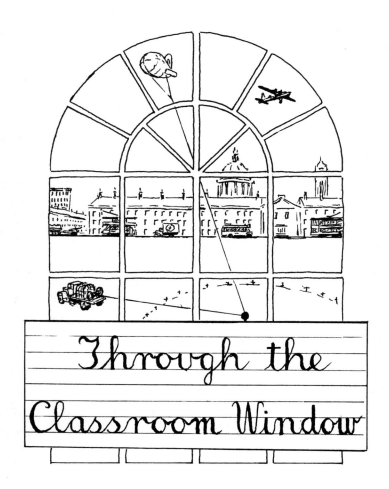

LIST OF PHOTOGRAPHS

All of these photographs are in the possession of U3A members who have given permission for their use in this book. They typify the children, the schools and the life and times of the 1920s, 30s and 40s.

INDEX